Where the
Light **Shines**
Through

Where the Light Shines Through

Discerning God in Everyday **Life**

Wes Avram

BrazosPress
Grand Rapids, Michigan

© 2005 by Wes Avram

Published by Brazos Press
a division of Baker Publishing Group
P.O. Box 6287, Grand Rapids, MI 49516-6287
www.brazospress.com

Printed in the United States of America

Library of Congress Cataloging-in-Publication Data
Avram, Wes, 1959-
    Where the light shines through : discerning God in everyday life / Wes Avram.
        p.   cm.
    Includes bibliographical references.
    ISBN 1-58743-088-6 (pbk.)
    1. Sermons, American—20th century. I. Title.
    BV4253.A88 2005
    252—dc22   2004018625

Contents

Enlightening Words

In the beginning there was nothing, formless void. Then God spoke a word, "Light," and there was. The land, plants, animals, us, all on the basis of nothing more than words. This is the way this God gets what God wants—words. There are other gods who, when they are in a creative mood, have coitus with other gods, or engage in cosmic battle between good and evil. This God just talks, speaks with sovereign majesty, says "Light," and there is light. Words precedes world.

In the beginning was the word, the word made flesh, God with us in the form of a preacher. In the Bible, everything good begins—whether it be creation or salvation—with words.

Wes Avram is good with words. For two decades he has been working the world with words—as college chaplain, seminary professor of preaching, and master preacher. Avram's God is a big talker, loquacious, self-revealing, but not in too simple or direct a way. Through this talk, God longs to communicate with us, but we, sinners as we are, can't always see the light shinning through the thickness of the mundane, the dullness of the ordinary, this veil of clay. So we need astute workers with words like Avram to show us what we have trouble seeing on our own, to, with words, tell us of the possibility that, despite our secular defenses, something's afoot.

In these essays the light shines through with gentleness, eloquence, and a serene confidence that God will talk to those who listen. Avram's theology is light on its feet, nimble, rooted in classical, orthodox Christianity but never dreary or somber. His voice, in these meditations, is beguiling, warm, and open, the sort of voice that doesn't have to argue, threaten, or plead because of his deep confidence that our God speaks, reaches, intrudes, and really means to redo Genesis 1 in us all over again with words.

You've got a cold heart and a dull mind if you read far into Avram's vivid essays without being startled by a flash of light or a gentle glimmer of enlightenment that proves a greater light determined to shine gloriously among us. When that happens, Avram's words have gotten to you, and you see, you believe you're new, and it's Genesis 1 all over again—light!

WILLIAM H. WILLIMON
RESIDENT BISHOP, BIRMINGHAM AREA
THE UNITED METHODIST CHURCH AND
FORMER CHAPLAIN OF DUKE UNIVERSITY

Introduction

God-Sensed

Danish philosopher Søren Kierkegaard said that you catch the tension of faith when you can hear the voice of God and the chiming of the hallway clock at the same instant. The chapters of this book circle about that tension. They are assured by the wager that the adventure of knowing God that we call the life of faith is given its texture by a full, divine sort of sensuality—God-sensed before God-known.

Christian thinkers tend to resolve Kierkegaard's tension theologically, by *comprehending* God. We interpret who God is and then describe what difference this makes for how we think about those chimes in the hallway. This theological comprehension usually follows a narrative something like this: God is the beginning and the end of all that is. We understand Jesus Christ to be the unity of beginning and end—Christ's Spirit tying God together in the shape of God's personality. Christ ties the narrative of God together both as a life story retold in history and as a continuing spiritual presence through history. This is how God is transcendent, wooing all of creation into the holy story of reconciliation, justice, and peace seen in the life of Jesus. God is immanent as we are inspired to identify ourselves with the main themes of this story and freely see ourselves as characters in it. We are to become, in effect, the thickness of the story's middle. This story of God (beginning, middle, and end), especially as it provides a role for us in its plot, is said to give life meaning. Many of our Sunday sermons, theological reflections, and strategies for Christian action spin out as interpretations of this story. The spinning is our *theo-logia*, our study and reasoning out of God.

Not bad for a day's work, except for a nagging problem. Though we may think of God this way, few if any of us sense or experience God this way. And we are in good company, for it also appears that no character in the Bible does either. The theological story of God is apt; it is even authoritative in certain ways. But I cannot feel it or smell it or taste it or hear it or even see it without an effort of reasoning and imagination. This God does not *happen*. This God is thought in a sort of composite picture gathered from accumulated fragments pasted together by logic. It is like the image of the heavens at night. Since scientists have posited the effect of light years, we know the constellations differently from the way we sense them. With light from stars reaching us at different intervals, we don't see the heavens about which astronomy teaches. We see an image of something that teaches us about what is, but the image we see never really was. Or think of the earth itself. I know it's round, but I experience it as flat.

Now don't get me wrong. I believe in theology, just as I believe the earth is round. That kind of knowledge can be a good corrective to limited and limiting experience. I just want to keep that kind of knowledge in its place. It takes good liturgy, decent preaching, fervent prayer, much singing, some laughter, shared compassion, and all grace to do just that.

I spent several years as the chaplain at a small college in the Northeast. In this work, I rarely had students wander into my office to tell me stories of experiencing the whole God whom the theological narrative describes. More often the stories were of disturbing brushes with God, or of upsetting and confusing glimpses of the sheer possibility of God, or of words heard in the night, or of the scent of a nascent life-commitment. These happenings were often surprising and sometimes frightening to those who experienced them. They were also sweet and welcoming. Their experiences came with intuitions of otherness, sometimes formed in church and sometimes not. These were partial and contingent sensations. The folks who had them sometimes came with a deep and inarticulate sense inspired from some source or another that there is something radically wrong and that things must turn in a new direction if they are to find life or if the world around them is to find hope. The experiencers wanted to interpret their experiences but were also afraid that by interpreting they might betray the very experiences they wanted to understand. They wanted to know but did not want to lose by knowing.

Our thinking can certainly include and respond to sense and perhaps be itself a kind of sense. Yet when we sense God, *God-sense* is other than an accomplishment of our thinking. God-sense comes *to* experience, passing by, happening in instants not yet grasped by theological vision. God-sense is like an event inserted into time, or as Jewish philosopher Emmanuel Levinas once wrote, like an "incision made in time which does not bleed."[1] It comes to the senses more like a rhythm than a theme, and it is worked out in the contingencies, confusions, and curiosities of our being. It can spin itself into a riff that can be recalled and almost repeated, but it begins in a movement that is sooner discovered than it is achieved—like the sweep of the divine tail before Elijah in front of the cave (1 Kings 19) or the tracing image of God in which we are created, a trace more like an echo than a resemblance in a mirror or the correspondence of a character trait (Genesis 1:26). God happens without beginning, middle, or end.

Consider the scent of incense or of Easter lilies, or the taste of new wine, or a supper with friends that becomes far more than dining, or the touch of healing, or the echoing in your bones of a compassion that evokes an unswerving sense of responsibility long before it is understood. These are images of how God comes to the senses. They are not God. They are traces of God. They are possibility, not necessity.

Immemorial and unimagined, God comes to experience like an unrecognizable stranger breaking down distinctions between the meaningful and the unfamiliar—perfectly unpredictable but not destructively so, and perfectly gracious but not gratuitous. Theology turns this stranger into a neighbor by building fences and throwing block parties. But the neighbor remains an *other* that such organizing can't fully control without harming.

Now there is in all of this that hazard I alluded to. You see, I don't want to naively equate God with just any experience of the senses. Just a glance at the world in which we live undercuts that equation. Our senses and experiences are too easily bought and sold like machine-made goods. Sometimes our souls are nearly consumed by a marketplace tyrannized by excitement and over-whelmed by options. The ways of sensing God that I am set-ting alongside theology are different altogether from religious experiences marketed like rock videos. The tension of faith I am describing holds experiences of God that are both more ordinary and more extraordinary than these.

Where are we with this sense of God-sense? Well, in addition to the quip with which I began, Kierkegaard also told a parable about how we experience God. It seems that the king of Denmark was being crowned in a ceremony of great pomp. There was music, majesty, and all of the honoraria one might expect on such an occasion. Just at the highest moment, a housekeeper appeared and began to clean—rags, buckets, and mop in tow. You see, she *always* polished the brass on Saturdays!

God's happening upsets any attempt to get ahold of it or control it. We respond with a chuckle or a frustrated question ("What?") or a pondering silence. Traces of God can be irreconcilable with our more thoughtful orderings of life. They demand more than genius of the intellect or good consumer taste. For alongside the liturgy, preaching, prayer, singing, laughter, love, and all grace I mentioned earlier, they also demand a certain emotional knack or a God-sensual savvy to be known for what they are and not taken for what they're not.

Let me suggest all of this in another way. Since 1993, I've had a piece of bark from a large and stately old red maple that stood tall in the campus quadrangle of Bates College. The tree was 150 years old, as old as the institution. It was so large that when chairs were set around it for outdoor festivities, the columns of marchers would move well apart—easily eight feet or more—to go around its base. In 1993, both the annual baccalaureate service and commencement ceremonies had been planned for the open area around this tree. A senior class rehearsal took place midafternoon on Saturday, the day before the baccalaureate service. Anxious and excited seniors lined up to rehearse their march into the seating area. Then, just ten minutes before the chairs would have been full of seniors, this tree suddenly crashed to the ground. Otherwise healthy, in full green leaf and a minute earlier looking no different from any other tree on the Quad, there lay this large and heavy tree, uprooted, flat on its side, crushing a quarter or more of the chairs. There was no warning; it was as if it were a perfectly normal event.

When I arrived shortly after it happened, people were already scurrying about, cutting the trunk with chain saws. Students were holding pieces of the chair they reckoned to have their number on it. Deans and chaplains, administrators and parents all wanted to be seen lending a hand by picking up a branch or two or more. Even the vice president for finance had his sleeves rolled up. Heavy equipment from the construction of the new dorm across campus was called in to cart away the bigger pieces. Students laughed nervously while standing together in the gaping hole the tree's roots had left behind, arms around each other as families and friends took pictures. A small souvenir exchange began with people sharing pieces of the tree and the mangled metal.

There was busyness everywhere around this tree. But private talk was in strangely quiet tones. Some simply stood and watched the event, waiting, smelling the air, taking it all in. Some whispered about deliverance and grace and smiled nervously at the immensity of it all. Others talked of luck. Some tried to find a scientific explanation. (Had it rained? No. How's the soil? Fine. How could the tree have been rotting inside while looking so healthy outside?) There were awkward jokes about God; one person described the falling as the "act of God on the Quad." Some were convinced that this was a wake-up call, as if it were a warning or a judgment from somewhere about something. One student thought it a message from a missing relative. But talk of the event itself, that if it had happened ten minutes later it would surely have left some graduating seniors dead and many injured, this talk was offered with a certain sensual awe confused by disbelief. While most conversations touched on the awful possibility, few could dwell on it.

By evening, the tree had been cleared away, the sod replaced, and a red maple sapling put in its place as a gift from the senior class. There was no trace left of the event, except in the little bit of remaining buzz and the stories on the six o'clock news. After all, like cleaning the brass, trees *always* fall on Saturdays. How strange how quickly we try to restore order after the surprising happenings of an ordinary world.

Into what narrative, in what theology, does this tree fall? Was it God, or was it nature? Was it an inconvenience, or a tragedy avoided by luck or grace? Looking at the Quad today, one could ask if it *was* at all. But it is sure that this experience evaded thought and explanation. It could only be sensed.

So it is with God, beyond theology. God happens like that tree. And we are left to respond. Where was God on the Quad? Neither in the falling nor in the sparing of lives. God was in the rhythm between the fall, the sparing, and the certain textures of response by which we all attended to the event—maybe. The tension of faith lies in simultaneously hearing the voice of God and the tree falling on the Quad, and sensing a rhythm between the two that lets us live in both without collapsing one into the other.

Admittedly, there is no reason to believe that either the collapse of a tree or the sparing of lives is associated with God at all. Some days, no trees fall on that quad. And other days, lives are tragically lost or irreparable harm is done within shouting distance of that very spot, for no good reason at all. The point is not to mystify experience. Nor is it to locate God in a particular place or time, necessarily. It is, first, to learn how to pay attention. There is no need to cover contingency so soon that sensation, or possibility, gets lost in manufactured normalcy—theological or otherwise. Theology tells us that God is always bigger than our experiences in time, however extravagant those experiences might be. If that is so, however, then it is also safe to say that God is never smaller.

And so we might consider Scripture. There God is generally not reduced to a conclusion or a proposition or a premise. Happening before being, God is *assumed* in Scripture. God is then responded to sensually and personally, and God is proclaimed concretely. Scripture bears God like we bear the curiosities and mysteries of people we begin to love because we sense their uniqueness in ways that delightfully, and in some ways frightfully, exceed our grasp. The Bible loves God. It does not prove God or defend God.

Do you know the old rabbinic tale of why God chose biblical Israel above all nations? The tale goes that God chose Israel because of all the nations to whom God offered the holy law, only Israel accepted God's offering before asking what the law said. Only Israel forged its relationship to God within the sensation of responsibility before the adventure of knowledge, according to this tale. "Here we are, Lord. Speak, your servant, Israel, is listening. Send us!"

Consider a story from the Gospel of John. Two disciples had been readied by John the Baptizer to sense the presence of the Christ when Christ arrived. But Jesus' arrival was curious. He had appeared the

day before, and John had identified him as the one they were waiting for, but the story doesn't say what transpired during the night.
What charge was in the air? What confusions over preparations and
actions? What directions now for John's ministry if Jesus is indeed
the one? We are simply moved to the next day, when Jesus passes
by again. "The Lamb of God," says John, pointing. And the two
disciples follow the scent. Jesus had not given a lecture and handed
out membership applications. He had simply passed by. They had
only a glimpse, a hint, and a reliable witness.

At some point, Jesus turns back and engages the two following him in a good rabbinic exchange, with questions answered
by questions in pursuit of a relationship to knowledge that can't
be separated from the experience of its discovery. "What are you
looking for?" he says, to begin his challenging query. And the
tension in the event is between the lines.

The text says that this was the tenth hour, which is about 4:00
p.m. And by the way the story unfolds, we might surmise it was
Friday, just before the Sabbath.

"What are you looking for?" Jesus asks.

The question is answered with a question that turns the attentiveness of the moment back on Jesus: "Master, where are
you staying?"

"Come and see," he replies. And they follow him in to spend
the Sabbath.

Jesus welcomes them into the tangible event that transforms
the search for meaning into an encounter with sense. He then
moves them toward the discovery of a calling.

Ask the questions that will take you deeper, not only into the
study or story of God but also into the happening of God, as if
invited to a Sabbath meal. And prepare yourself for the results!

I knew an Englishman I'll call Reggie. He told me of an event
that still puzzled him. I knew Reggie to be an intelligent and committed person in general, but in telling me this story he appeared

more aware and attentive than usual, full of consciousness and sensation. Now Reggie had for some time been an active member of the SWSO (called Sweezo), the Socialist Workers Student Organization in Britain. His membership in this organization was a well-considered expression of his theologically formed commitment to social justice. One afternoon (maybe a Saturday cleaning day), he was handing out revolutionary pamphlets to folks in line at the local unemployment office—recruiting for the revolution. Handing out one after another, he was halted by a woman holding a child tugging at her shirt. "I don't want your pamphlet," the woman told him. "I want your *attention*. Here! I want to *talk* to you. I need *you*." Reggie tried to get away to continue handing out his pamphlets. But the woman pulled him back and looked him in the eyes, breaking through his nerve. (It was now time for the brass to be polished.) Reggie pulled himself away and moved down the line, only to turn and see the woman still looking. He walked back.

"What are you looking for?"

The woman seemed to answer by asking where Reggie's heart resided.

Reggie told me that he had not handed out a pamphlet since. He dropped his pile right there, gave the woman his telephone number, and began helping with shopping, errands, and the other challenges of living as an unemployed single mother. He met the woman's friends. He found himself helping them as well. And a new kind of living began. Reggie began to feel differently about many aspects of his own living. And he knew he was learning to hear the voice of God.

Now, lest you declare the wrong sort of victory here, know that Reggie never really changed his politics. He remained as committed as ever to revolution, but his sense of revolution, both theologically and politically, was expanded beyond imagining. The Holy Spirit was doing something far newer in him than simply changing his beliefs. The Spirit was inserting a texture of responsiveness in him and a readiness to hear that was more like faith than theme. His was a new method for a different purpose.

God happens like that, not first of all in opposition to grand narratives or theological visions but in the midst of them—upsetting, awakening, making sense. This happening is a touching of sorrow, a hearing of the word, a tasting of food prepared by another, a smelling of who knows what, a seeing of the marks of glory in what we normally consider to be ordinary.

In talking of these sensual implications of the call of God, mystic Evelyn Underhill put it this way: "His call is very simple, but so very exacting. The response is equally clear. 'Send me' doesn't exactly mean, 'I'm going that way anyhow. Is there anything I can do for you?' It means the delicate balance between freedom and surrender, that self-oblivious zest which is the salt of the Christian: will and grace acting together on ever higher levels of cooperative action."[2]

That "self-oblivious zest," tensed by the simultaneous experience of grace and will, is the experience of God-*sensed*. It is the inescapable companion to God-thought I've been describing. And it is the sort of savvy for religion I mentioned earlier. The term *wisdom* might also apply. And more urgent still, this may be what the church calls *hope*. It is like dogs tracking through a forest of tempting smells, still able to search out that one scent that makes the hunt. The hope that opens us to a sense of God is a focused attention and a responsiveness. It is the rhythm—calling, and enlivening.

Perhaps you'll sense such hope by gently and confidently learning which life-giving scents to follow among the many poisonous ones swirling about. Perhaps you'll sense it in the places where all-too-easy interpretations of the world crack apart. Perhaps you'll taste it in the church—in nourishing worship, in shared Eucharist, in mission to reach out, or in the spiritual sustenance of good and just work. Perhaps it will resonate in the words of trustworthy others or in the echoes of your own spirit's yearning for more. Many know this way of hope and know it in the one theological premise that is greater than the ways any theology can interpret it: God happens, by God's grace, even to us.

This book wanders about in this hope and waits on this Spirit. It is divided into three sections, according to three realms where God-sense is promised us. The first of these realms is that space in a believer's soul where the human spirit and the Holy Spirit do their business together. In "The Heartbeat of Hope," I claim that Christian spirituality has a rhythm not unlike a heartbeat moving between power and peace. In the second chapter, called "God Then . . . ," I borrow the imagery of a poem by Denise Levertov and a teenager's insight at a Christmas pageant in Maine to poetically describe the powerful peace Christ's Spirit promises in that space of holy business in our souls. In "Unpaid Internship," I ask what is truest about our lives when we sense this spiritual rhythm. And in "Only by Hearsay," I think about the ancient story of Job and his family as a way of exploring that truth more deeply.

The second of these realms is found by looking at the many ways in which the intrigues of the world and the movement of Christ's Spirit meet. God-sense has a more political feel here, found in the real struggles of social life. In "Jury Duty in the New Realm," I think about the truly radical implications of the phrase Christians pray so often in the Lord's Prayer, "Thy kingdom come," in light of a story Jesus told. In "Ringmaster Ned," I let the story of the last week of Jesus' life become a parable for how he might be active in the world today. In "9/12 Living in a 9/11 World," I assume the image of Christ's action in the world from "Ringmaster Ned" and wonder out loud about what comes of trust when terror and confusion rule the day. In "No Wilder Peace," I reinterpret an often-read passage from the book of Isaiah in order to find a way to understand courageous, Spirit-filled action in the world. Three stories from present-day Israel and Palestine serve as examples.

The third realm of this promise is the one that should perhaps be the first—the church. The heartbeat of power and peace that gives texture to the Spirit's work inside us and in the world is protected and nourished by the church. Believing that, I offer four appeals to the church to pay closer attention to the Spirit in her midst. The first chapter in this section, "Blinded by the Light," acknowledges the frustration felt by so many churchgoers when the most pressing question they bring to church is blithely neglected by preachers: "Is it *true*?" I believe it *is* true and that it is good news—enough to change the church, enough to change the world, and enough to change our hearts. The next chapter, "Against Heroes," is a modest appeal to consider what this news might mean for how Christians think about leadership. An argument among Jesus' closest followers frames this reflection. The appeal in "On Martin Luther King Jr.: Self-Dispense or Self-Defense," is to remember how thoroughgoing the New Testament call to nonviolence really is and to begin to reimagine the church in earshot of that call. "Gifts That Work" is an appeal in the form of a meditation on how differently we might think about the church if we believed that when we pray for the kingdom, we are praying for a way of ordering our lives together so that we don't count costs before we give love. This is how God happens.

The book's epilogue is an extended note on Christian preaching in light of all of this. When preaching goes well, its force unites these three realms and takes them to the edge of what these chapters try to describe. It is one of the most reliable ways by which Christians make sense of God. Even more than that, it is one of the ways in which Christians believe God happens. The church clings to the possibility that the Holy Spirit can happen in special, even unique, ways in the four-way transaction among Scripture, speaker, congregation, and Spirit called preaching. This epilogue might be of special interest to pastors and theology students, but it is written for anyone who wants to make God-sense of this—preachers and hearers alike. Much of what I have written in this introduction might suggest that the worship of the church, centered as it mostly is around the preached Word and shared sacraments, may not be the first place God happens. Preaching is so full of theology, after all, and too often falls into crass emotionalism when it attempts to get out of its head. So little preaching tends to strike a good balance. Yet by concluding the book with a note on preaching, I mean to resist that implication. We bring our whole selves and all our experiences to worship, when we worship—chiming clocks, falling trees, polishing brass, unemployment lines, and all. We bring our experience into the reverberation of Christian proclamation. It makes good sense to think about how all of this might work. For in that odd place where hearing, rendering, and yearning converge we can learn the habits of attentiveness that shape our sense of God everywhere else.

Part 1

Sensing the Spirit

The Heartbeat of Hope

Revelation 21:1–22:7

If you ever travel to Atlanta and find yourself on the campus of Emory University, walk over to the Candler School of Theology. Candler is Emory's divinity school. You will find there a chapel complex designed by Paul Rudolph. It was dedicated in 1981. There are a couple of distinguishing, and controversial, features of Rudolph's design. Quite to the contrary of the visions of worship and Christian community that have informed the design of most Christian sanctuaries, the Cannon Chapel is built as an empty box. There are no permanent furnishings. All pieces are movable—the seats, the pulpit, the all-in-one-unit pipe organ, and the cross that can be hung over the balcony railing wherever it suits a liturgical purpose. Here is a view of worship and gathering as a movable and flexible feast. Yet it also feels unsettling, as though things that happen there are fleeting.

If you look outside of the chapel, you do see, as you might expect, a cross on top marking it as a place of Christian worship and study. But following the vision that produced the inside of the chapel, the cross is not at the top of a steeple standing up into the air proclaiming the triumph of God over death and declaring the sovereignty of God over all of society. Instead, the cross is etched out of negative space, as though hidden from the world. You see a rounded slab of stone bolting up toward the heavens, as if it were a tablet or a door or a barrier between your vision and the sky. Inside the stone, you see a cross-shaped opening. This is a cross carved or dug into the stuff of the world, not laid over the top.

One glance at this cross sees an embarrassed and hidden thing, shy before the onslaught of secular culture and retiring to a place where it can hardly be seen. It appears to betray the historic glory of the cross. Yet another glance sees what the early mothers and fathers of the church saw when they spied cross-shaped marks everywhere they looked, whether in nature or the chance effect of human hands—a cross in the grain of a door, the branches of a tree, a shell, a stone. In any cruciform pattern they saw signs of God's glory, similar to the way they spied signs of the Trinity in the natural divisions of human speech or physical objects into threes. Their eyes would see in the Candler chapel cross a signal that God's glory is revealed to anyone who has eyes to see but won't impose itself on those not yet ready.

The Bible ends a bit like that Candler cross. In its ending lies a startling image of what comes to be the very heartbeat of biblical faith and Christian hope: the new Jerusalem of Revelation 21. Between the Candler cross and that passage lies the meeting of yearning and history that coalesces into the image of a new city replacing the old and descending from heaven as though the gift of a new start, a rebooting of the world in a Jerusalem marked neither by pain nor death. This is a city without tears or mourning, in which our relationship with the Creator is without confusion. God is our God, and we are God's people, with results that change the way we order our world. Here is the yearning one might call the systolic beat of faith, characterized in terms of a biblical peace in which compassion, forgiveness, and justice kiss without doing violence to the very world God would liberate. And there lies yet another yearning bound to this rhythm, in what one might call faith's diastolic beat. This beat complements that first systolic beat. This second beat is doxology—all praise to God. For here we see the new Jerusalem descending from heaven not only as a material dream of just peace (*shalom*) in a sin-ridden and broken world but as a crown descending on the head of Jesus. This very Jesus is the sacrificial lamb sitting on the throne of God, ready to be named the sovereign of all creation. He is hidden from the foundation of the world, yet revealed in glory through his suffering on behalf of the world.

That's the flow of imagery in this chapter of Revelation, with jeweled streets connoting the precious stones of the crown and the shining face of Jesus being the light that replaces the temple as the residence of God within the city walls. Christian hope takes both of these beats into a rhythm of deep longing dug into the stuff of the world and glorious satisfaction in the prospect that Jesus reigns. It is a reality the world does not yet see and we only begin to know. Here resides the spirituality and the hope that empower Christian love.

See Mother Teresa reframing the challenge a news reporter makes to her during the Israeli invasion of Beirut. Under the rain of bombs, she is removing children from a war-torn hospital for the developmentally disabled. The reporter asks her if she thinks her efforts are enough, given that there is another hospital in Beirut with another hundred such children. She does not answer, except to say, "Don't you think it is a good thing to help these little ones?" And the reporter asks her again about her plans for the other hospitals and whether her efforts can be counted as successful with the other children unattended. She responds again, not with anger or frustration but with what Robert Inchausti calls "immovable determination." "I think it is a good thing to help these children," she says. Inchausti continues, "And then as her shoulder sank beneath the weight of the stretcher, she gave the reporter a glance that asked, 'Why don't you help me lift these children into the ambulance; that is something you can do.' It was one of those rare moments . . . when the confusions of the world were defeated, if only for a moment, by a practical act of love."[1]

So the systolic beat: there is no more powerful, and finally more realistic, force in the world than a desire for God's reign against all appearances to the contrary.

And so the diastolic beat: there is no more potent a maker of peace, in our own souls and between people, than an acceptance that God's reign has already been accomplished, even as we desire it.

When you can breathe out, finally, and say, "God is all in all," you can begin to find the freedom required to live in a world in which you are, because of evil and whimsy and self-destructive ways, not really free at all.

"God reigns!" And the world changes for us from the inside out.

"God reigns!" And we are finally free to act on what we know and change for good.

"God is all in all!" And the cross finally reveals more than it hides.

God reigns! Now what more can we say? Let me begin by taking a stab at what we *cannot* say. First, when the church says that God is all in all, it is not saying that God is the great fixer of evil or whimsy or our self-destructive ways. Now don't get this wrong. By some mystery, it appears rock-solid true that God does fix things sometimes, and that the God who is worshiped is a miracle-working Spirit in the world. It *is* the case, it appears, that sometimes all of creation rallies to the aid of a person who prays. And yet this does not *always* happen. Jesus himself asserts in Scripture that the rain falls on the just as well as the unjust (Matt. 5:45). We are all subject to the arbitrariness of nature, the random banality of evil, and the sometimes uncontrollable aspects of our own willfulness or the tyranny of others. Even as we triumph, we're also victims, and even as victims, we can yet victimize others.

So let there never be preached a theology so glib as to imply that as long as Air Jesus has got the ball, it's okay if we're down in the fourth period. For the waters of God's providential care are much deeper, choppier, and more life-giving. For rather than simply winning at the buzzer, God's sovereignty sometimes changes the game. And *this* is what prompts Christian praise.

Faith has power, yes, but it is not magic. Magic moves in one direction, from its user toward the thing it affects. The mystery of faith always moves in many directions, affecting everything. For God is always doing more than one thing. Which is why when the church prays, it prays for specific things even while it prays for openness to whatever Christ's Spirit will do. It's the heartbeat, you see.

And so, second, when the church says that God reigns it is not saying that there is an understandable reason for everything that happens. There may be reasonable explanations or describable causes for events, but God's control is not the control of a puppeteer, guiding and manipulating. God relates *to* creation and *within* creation but does not *overpower* creation. And so here's another mystery.

Folks try to resolve this mystery in one of two ways, each of which finally fails. Some decide that there is some reason for everything that happens and find comfort in the hope that they'll sort it out in the end. Others decide that all is chance and that God makes a nice principle of unity but is rather ineffective in real time. But neither of these options fits biblical faith, for while God does act directly once in a while (for which one might give thanks),

God's reason is not, first, a reason that *causes* events. It is first a reason that works in the midst of events. There is not so much a reason for things, in this sense, as there is a reason, or better a reasoning, in and through things.

Scott Jones, for many years the Episcopal chaplain at Northwestern University, used to say that salvation resides not in why but in what—not "Why me?" or "Why us?" or "Why this?" but "What, God, are you doing in me, in us, in this?"

And so, third, when the church boldly asserts that God is in control, it is not saying that it fully understands what this means or has on demand some source of secret knowledge. Quite the contrary. To affirm in our hearts that God is in the midst of the moment and remains faithful past rejection is to feel that second beat of Christian faith and hope in the deepest of ways. For unless there is an element of praise in our prayer, it is not God to whom we pray. And unless there is a sense in which the Holy Spirit knows better than we what is true, it is not the Holy Spirit from whom we learn.

This truth is tough for well-schooled folk who are used to defining God at their whim. We mold God into the shape of what seems to us reasonable and moral. But the Holy Spirit searches God's heart far more effectively than we, and God's glory begins inside God rather than inside our theologies. We sense that glory; we don't create it. It creates us, even through the more difficult stuff of life.

Christina Feldman and Jack Kornfield write of a story drawn from a physician's memoirs.[2] It seems a young man in his early twenties was diagnosed with a rare form of bone cancer. After extensive treatment, the cancer took his leg clear up to his hip. Long, arduous therapy with crutches and an artificial leg gave way to a negotiated compromise with mobility and the modicum of a normal life. During therapy the physician occasionally asked his patient to draw images of his feelings. Once, the patient handed him an image of a delicate vase, cracked. The crack had been drawn and redrawn to the point of nearly tearing the paper, deepening a chasm right down the center of the otherwise perfect object. A heart, or a spirit, broken.

It was hard work for this young man to reconcile himself to this new reality. Slowly, however, humor became therapeutic. And a change began. The doctor writes of a time when the young man visited the hospital room of a woman in her twenties who had just undergone a double mastectomy for breast cancer. It was her birthday, and so the young man turned up the radio, removed his limb, took the woman by the hand, and began to jump about the room in dancing motions, turning pain into laughter. Eventually the nurses and other staff on the floor joined in and the room was transformed.

Somewhere along this path the young man repeated an abiding yes to God and accepted a new life based solely and fully on God's provision for him. No false promises. No thin dreams or recklessness. Only true hope and openness to the gift of each moment as a sacred trust from the One who sits, alpha and omega, at the heart of the world.

The story concluded years later when the physician and the young man, by then no longer so young, met again. The doctor opened his files and pulled out the drawing of the vase. And the artist of this broken vase took the portrait in his hands and stared for what seemed the longest time.

"This isn't finished," he said, and took up a pencil. Through tearing eyes, he added something. "Now it's complete," he said and turned it back to the doctor. He had drawn rays of light shining from inside of the vase.

He said, "Now I know that the crack is where the light shows through."

As the church takes its yearning for a new world mapped by justice, forgiveness, and compassion and shapes that yearning into a crown suitable for the head of Christ, we may see our faith mature. We may move from youthful visions toward a seasoned hope in the knowledge that God *is* all in all. We may begin to see that the chinks in the armor of our planned and managed lives—while ever cracks—may also be the very carved out crosses through which the light shows. They are the jeweled streets of a new Jerusalem.

2

God Then . . .

Luke 2

Those who lived in a land of deep darkness—on them light has shined.

ISAIAH 9:2 NRSV

God then,
encompassing all things, is
defenseless? Omnipotence
has been tossed away, reduced
to a wisp of damp wool?
And we,
frightened, bored, wanting
only to sleep till catastrophe
has raged, clashed, seethed and gone by without us,
wanting then

to awaken in quietude without remembrance of agony,
we who in shamefaced private hope
had looked to be plucked from fire and given
a bliss we deserved for having imagined it,

   is it implied that we
must protect this perversely weak
animal, whose muzzle's nudgings
suppose there is milk to be found in us?
Must hold to our icy hearts
a shivering God?

So be it.
Come, rag of pungent
quiverings,
dim start.
   Let's try
if something human still
can shield you,
      spark
of remote light.

DENISE LEVERTOV[1]

One year I was asked to emcee the Christmas Eve children's pageant at a local church. I agreed, foolhardily. Now this church in Maine had had a rough time with live baby Jesuses over the years, with infants scheduled for performance getting sick, nervous mothers having a hard time letting go, spit-ups and weeping and wailing. In the year I'm remembering, the problem wasn't colic or coughing. It was that there were no babies to be had. A two-year-old just wouldn't do. The pastor assumed they'd use a doll.

I arrived in the afternoon for rehearsal. There was fifteen-year-old Roxanne, dressing for her part as Mary. She slowly became transformed. Her jeans, T-shirt, and roughly thrown-together hair pulled back gave way to a wrapping robe, faux Middle Eastern head cover, and flowing youthful hair. Someone handed her a well-worn plastic baby in a polyester blanket.

"Oh, I don't like this at all," she said. And the pageant director began to explain the lack of productivity in the congregation that year.

She said, "Oh, that's okay. I'm not sure I'd want a live one either. Can I have a few minutes? I have an idea." And she disappeared into the church kitchen, to return a couple of minutes later with a flashlight and a piece of thin, rough, eggshell-colored woolen cloth. She wrapped the cloth over the top of the light and turned it on. "Hmm, that's not right either. Looks like I'm trying to light the cloth on fire. Hmm." And she disappeared again.

She returned from the church parlor with a small lampshade. With wonder, I watched her mind at work. She stuck the flashlight in the little metal brackets inside the shade and aimed the light out the top. Then she wrapped the woolen cloth around the shade and over her arm, her hand holding the flashlight at just the right angle. She flipped it on. "There you are," she said, "baby Jesus." No time to challenge her decision, and no one wanted to question a youth anyway. So it passed.

Come the evening pageant. In the darkened sanctuary the effect was eerie. Up on the stage, buried a little away from view, surrounded by sixteen-year-old Joseph, three nine-year-old shepherds, and a five-year-old lamb, Mary held her light—glowing, shining up with its own source of energy, gently, almost imperceptibly, but still noticeably illuminating the figures in the makeshift manger.

> So be it.
> Come, rag of pungent
> quiverings,
> dim start.
>   Let's try
> if something human still
> can shield you,
>   spark
> of remote light.

A dear teacher of mine, Ivan Illich, once said that the ancients didn't see light. By this he meant that what we mean when we speak of seeing light was an unconceived notion in the world of Jesus' day and before, and even for quite a while after. We say light and think of rays or waves or beams that bounce, projected from a source of fire called the sun or from some little imitation like a candle. The composition of surfaces struck by rays of light absorbs certain rays but not others, which accounts for how things appear to us in their textures and colors. I'm no physicist, but I do know that the light we see today is this light, the physicists' light.

The light Isaiah saw, which gave the image of the child coming as light in the darkness and which was seen by all who called Jesus the Light of the World, was not a physicist's light. It was more like Roxanne's light. It was an illumination emanating from the inside and meeting other emanations to create something more.

Isaiah's light didn't bounce, you see. Isaiah's light didn't even reflect. Isaiah's light—the light that was promised the darkness, the light that no darkness can put out, the light that is the Light of the World—commingled with creation.

Light was a power that gave life and participated in life. And even life—so filled by light and sound and heart and promise—was other than an idea of biology. Life-light shone deep, broad, and in ever-fragile ways. It was contingent light, dependent on powers not so predictable as our science makes known. And yet powerful still.

Each thing has its own light, said the Greeks. That light comes from inside it and moves out into common space. In such space, images or rays of vision from each participating thing meet and mix and mingle their way into illumination.

To say that the light that will shine in the darkness is the Light of the World known to us as Jesus is to say that Jesus shines like the light that Isaiah spied and Mary knew. He does not glance off the surface of things to give them texture or color. He comes up and through and fills from the center outward. He meets us in the middle spaces, in between, creating something new in the meeting as we mingle with his light on our own way to illumination.

This Light that no darkness can put out is dependent on no sun. It meets even that source of light and fills it too. This Light illumines all people—hidden within, surrounded, shielded, protected sometimes. We might think we can flick it on and off at our will, but we cannot. It has its own will. It is finally other than what we think it is. This Light, Jesus.

Spark of a remote Spirit, commingling with God-begetting whom we've called Father, and God-begotten whom we've called Son, in the very world that the Holy Spirit—God-becoming—created from darkness and void. Not unlike the occasional darkness and void of our own spirits, waiting as they may be for this illumination. Wait, as you pray, for this.

Spark of a remote hope, commingling with our deepest fears and thinnest dreams with power to reshape them, if we'll let them be reshaped, into ways of living that are more firmly and faithfully drawn than what we could ever imagine if left to ourselves. Live in this light, and open your eyes to things you can now see in ways you've never seen before. Like waking up to a morning star.

Spark of a remote release, the end of banging against objects that are opaque before searching eyes. Move in this light and you can begin to see through. The world becomes softer even as you can face its hardness, for the first time, without threat or terror. Peace at last in this light. And courage again to move into your living, no matter where you find it, with the glowing awareness, like from inside the manger, that you *can* live right and well. You can live finally free of false battles. You are no longer bound.

A little light inside a lampshade, covered by cloth from the wool of a lamb, held tenderly, like a baby. Unusual view from the balcony.

> God then,
> encompassing all things, is
> defenseless? Omnipotence

has been tossed away, reduced
to a wisp of damp wool? . . .

So be it.
Come, rag of pungent
quiverings,
dim start.
    Let's try
if something human still
can shield you,
        spark
of remote light.

3

Unpaid Internship

Matthew 9:35–10:23

The preacher stood in the pulpit of Morningside Baptist Church on the south side of Atlanta and began his eulogy: "Jack had arrived that morning as he had every morning, before anyone else, to sweep the floors, start the coffee, thaw the beef patties, pull a couple dozen loaves of bread out of the big refrigerator, and more. When the volunteers and other staff showed up an hour later he unlocked the doors with his usual smile. He greeted us with the same words he had every morning: 'Ah, my friends, the harvest is plentiful, but the workers are few. Ask the Lord of the harvest, therefore, to send out workers into his harvest field.' And we all nodded in agreement."

Now, I knew Jack. I was one of those volunteers. I worked with him for a few weeks in a church basement soup kitchen in center-city Atlanta. The kitchen served hundreds of guests each day—street people and other folks down on their luck or caught in cycles of despair and self-destruction. Jack had been a guest in the kitchen himself a while before, back when he had been bouncing between sleeping in the park and renting cheap hotel rooms when he could put a few dollars together.

Yes, I knew Jack. And I liked him. We used to call him Captain because he sometimes wore an old captain's uniform he may have picked up in some used-clothing store. I seem to recall his mentioning army days.

The captain was a good man. Gentle. Helpful. He showed hardwon compassion for others, born I'm sure of the many times in his life when he needed compassion himself—and, I'm guessing, when he didn't get what he needed.

One day in the kitchen a man pulled out a knife. The captain was there before anyone knew it; he neutralized the situation and had the knife without hurting anyone, including the man with the knife.

It turned out that unbeknownst to those with whom he so faithfully worked in that soup kitchen, the captain was as pivotal and faithful a worker at Morningside Baptist. He was an usher every Sunday and a tireless helper with church fellowship and ministries to folks in need. Through hard times and slightly better times, the captain made a difference.

So I knew the captain—or at least I'd watched him for a few weeks. And I can tell you that in my experience the captain was not a man of many words, nor was he a man given to quoting Scripture. I do not remember him saying what the eulogist told us he said that morning as he greeted us, "Ah, my friends, the harvest is plentiful, but the workers are few." No. The captain had been as quiet as he had been every morning. But it was that morning that led to the odd and wonderful funeral day at Morningside Baptist Church when a sanctuary was packed with black folks from the south side, white folks from the north side, and a summer seminarian like myself. It was that morning, you see, that the captain collapsed and died while lying on the pastor's couch. That morning, like the other mornings I can recall, he just smiled as we entered. That's all.

So maybe the preacher lied.

Yet I think you know, from what little you know about the captain, that when it's all summed up and a little value is added from those last few years when his life got back together, and when all the contradictions are resolved in the face of the Christ he claimed, there was no such lie in that old captain's life: the harvest *was* plentiful and his kind of labor was hard to find. There was no better way to describe what his life said, and what each ounce of his being finally meant, than for that eulogist to put words in his mouth that day.

Now, imagine being at the cocktail hour before an auction for public television. You overhear someone talking about you, borrowing words from the Gospel of Matthew to describe your life. "Let me tell you," he says, "as she goes about, she proclaims the Good News, 'The kingdom of heaven has come near.' She cures the sick, raises the dead, cleanses the lepers, casts out demons. She knows she received without payment, so she gives without payment, keeping nothing in the bank for a rainy day. I mean, she takes no gold or silver or copper coins stitched into a belt, no bag for her journey, or second tunic or sandals or a staff, for she believes her labor is worth the support she gets from her fellow travelers, and she is confident she will receive what she needs. Like a sheep among wolves, yet nobody's fool. Wise as a serpent, yet innocent like a dove."

The person saying this may well be lying. And yet when it's all summed up, with a little value added from whichever good years you choose, and with all your contradictions resolved in the face of the Christ you claim, is it really a lie?

In Matthew's Gospel, one hears about fields ripe for harvest. The image resonates with nearly every description of Christian ministry. It has had direct influence on our historic understand-ings of ordained, or what some call professional, ministry. And it has had an equally marked effect on images of the ministries into which the church pretends to send everyone who is baptized.

Jesus says to his disciples, "I am sending you out like sheep into the midst of wolves; so be wise as serpents and innocent as doves" (Matt. 10:16 NRSV). And the implication of this can be stated with uncomfortable clarity: "You will be handed over and flogged. You will be dragged before governors and kings because of Jesus. How else will they know about him? When they hand you over, however, you needn't worry about how you are to speak or what you are to say, for what you are to say will just be given to you at the time." And the Gospel of Matthew is direct: "It is not you who speak. It will be God speaking through you" (v. 20).

"And if all goes well," to paraphrase the Gospel even more, "you'll leave a lot of upset in your wake! You'll split apart families. Brothers and sisters will mess each other up because one will go and 'get religion' because of you, sell his part of the family time-share and leave to serve the poor. And you'll break parents' hearts when the kids forego law school for seminary because of what you preach. And what a brilliant political career they could have had if not for you!"

"So you won't always be liked," Jesus says. "And when things get unduly hard for you in one town because of this, don't get overanxious or beat yourself over the head. There's plenty to do elsewhere. You don't own anything anyway, so go on to the next town where there's probably just as much need and maybe a little more openness" (vv. 21–25).

Who among us? I try, but I think it's been a while since I set a brother against a brother or, for that matter, a parent against a child. How many among the baptized love so recklessly?

Though there *was* Peter. I could write about Peter, a young person who rather proved the rule by exception. He was a bright and, in many ways, winsome college student. He used to make the rounds between the offices of three or four adults on campus to share with each of us a bit of his wranglings over all manner of cosmic things. He decided to read the New Testament at one point, and he made the mistake of taking it seriously. Its nagging call to compassion stuck. He started doing all sorts of things on campus to help people in tough times. Things got a little rough, however, when he picked up a tired and rather sad young drifter at a truckstop on his way home for Thanksgiving. Things got chilly between Peter and his family that Thanksgiving. But not to worry, Peter was just a rebellious adolescent. He makes no claim on the rest of us! Except, of course, for the possibility that Jesus might have done the very thing he did.

Yet there *are* those helpful and faithful and generous and caring and mercy-proclaiming and hope-making and God-honoring things that you also do, now and then. Very important, those things, and surely inspired by the courage the Holy Spirit gives us when we ask and are willing to receive. But the Scriptures push on those things too. For alongside the good things we do, there remains an even more dangerous extravagance in the kind of life to which the church keeps saying the gospel calls the baptized. We are called to a kind of living that is attentive to the world around us in ways we just can't sustain without God. And we are called to a generosity that is so free that it exposes our habit of hedging our bets. And we are called to a way of seeing miracles at work that belies ordinary logic. This is a wisdom and a willingness to let go of control in ways that challenge our need to cling. It questions our habits of waging the wrong battles. It is an urgency that interrupts our distractions. And it is a fearlessness that shames those worries that usually fill our days.

The church has always said we should mold our lives in the image of the people Jesus sent out with those words about the harvest. And the church has always wanted to believe that this is exactly its own role in the world. And the odd and wonderful thing about this is that even though few people live like this, and though the church also fails the vision, all may yet be mended in Christ. For like the captain, when the pieces are added up and all is completed in the face of Christ, such free compassion and gracious living *is* accomplished, even in us. And life *is* perfect in Christ—again, despite how broken life may seem.

And so the contradiction between the lives we live—however noble and compassionate and faith-seeking they may be—and the demand the Bible seems to place on us. The contradiction will be just too great, and the nervous laughter it brings just too close, if you don't, in fact, let the Spirit hold it. Let worship bring out power to acknowledge it, and let God's grace give you enough space to knock around in it a bit without feeling like you have to either deny the contradiction altogether or somehow explain it away. It is far too easy to look at the demands of the gospel on Christian lives and either dismiss them as irrelevant, ignore them for fear they're too radical, or settle for a chronic sense of failure. Yet Christian living is said to bring joy.

The answer, so the Scriptures seem to say, is not found in explaining away, ignoring, or compromising such high demands. The answer, rather, is to seek the truth about our lives and then tell that truth. The answer is to confess the contradictions we find—to God, to ourselves, and to the church. And the answer is to be unembarrassed by the contradictions and to never cease wanting more than what our own efforts can give us. And the answer is finding in that back and forth between our honesty and our yearning a desire and a readiness for the Christ's Spirit to come. Notice the contradictions. Let them be, just long enough to let Christ's Spirit fill them. And then watch how the movement between your yearning for more in life and the good that Christ can give begins to heal the contradictions and show you new ways to live.

The Spirit may nudge you to dramatic action to heal the rift, perhaps to the dismay of others. The same Spirit may also nudge in more private, quieter ways. The Spirit allows us to count as joy the grace that holds us as we mine the depths of what our spirits strive in us to live out—as individual believers and as Christ's church—in quiet service to each other and in support of ministries that make a difference; in careful study and in hard-nosed determination to know more than what the world would use to blind us; in the desire to know more of how the world really works, what God is really doing, and where we, together, are really called to give witness to love; in prayer; in hope; in the courage to receive as well as give; and most assuredly in the confidence that the eulogist's words do not lie but tell a deep truth when they tell the story of the captain who is opening the doors as we, the volunteers, arrive each day, saying to us, "Ah, the harvest is plentiful indeed."

4

Only by Hearsay

The Book of Job

Before, I knew you only by hearsay but now, having seen you with
my own eyes . . .

JOB 42:5 NJB

With apologies to readers who work in advertising, I must
confess that one of my hobbies in college was making up
ad campaigns. One that I was particularly proud of was
an idea for a Xerox pitch when photocopying was first becoming
commonplace. I called it, "If Xerox had been there . . ."

Imagine a room full of monks, eyes bleary, shaking off the
soreness of their arms after hours of transcribing manuscripts
of the Bible (sometimes with mistakes, by the way), snipping at
each other from exhaustion. Over in a back room, unnoticed, is a
smirky-faced novice, relaxed, feet up on the table, sipping a Coke
and leafing through a completed manuscript he just pulled off of

his trusty, if oversized, photocopier. Or imagine Aaron coming up to Moses just after the blocks on which God has etched the Ten Commandments have been broken. "Don't worry, Moses, we have a copy tablet. And we've made some brochures to distribute to avoid those nasty misunderstandings that can come with oral transmission. It's really much better this way."

Ah, if Xerox had been there . . .

And if we'd had such technologies during Jesus' ministry? Flysheets at all his rallies, cleverly tailored for each generation and each audience. Instant reproductions of his words through taped recordings or photocopied notes. We'd be all set. These days you can imagine him doing live streaming over the Internet. No need to deal with the inconvenience of memory or the unreliable shaping of the story by an early community of believers. We could grasp it and control it, getting the stuff right. We could turn our theologizing into a kind of Sunday morning *Jerusalem Week in Review*, with church leaders as pundits giving their opinions on one or another video clip of Jesus' dealings with the world. We could avoid the messiness of the Gospel stories altogether.

In the literate, and now postliterate, culture in which most readers of this book live it's easy to expect instant access to facts. We can recap, revise, and review in order to nail things down. We can instantly correct if we need to. Folks record and dub, photograph and photocopy, digitally remaster and edit. We consume words and ideas in hopes that the volume of easy repetition, criticism, evaluation, commentary, and assessment will suffice for discovering truth. This is not unlike other ways in which we try to make religion plain. In an age of electronic reproduction, it is easy to assume that religion, too, should be accessible at first glance. It's easy to insist it be a bit simplistic (though not simple) and easily manipulated to suit special needs. We are all coming to share an unspoken assumption that a quick glance suffices for information and that processed knowledge suffices for wisdom.

Now, I shouldn't deny that sometimes you *can* catch something with a quick glance that you miss on close examination. You can sometimes see the forest despite the trees when you step back to a certain vantage point. I believe this. We should take those quick-glance big-picture looks when we can. But we shouldn't stay there too long. For you see, sometimes you can get certain truths and possibilities and wonderful surprises in life only from a good long hike up and through them and by discovering things in them that just can't be copied. Like a good long marriage, I suppose, or a lifetime of studying, praying, arguing, wrestling, hearing, reading, and playing with Scripture, or a life of living with the person, presence, and work of Christ's Spirit in your life. Sometimes there's no substitute for sitting down, finding the leisure and good company with which to think and think again, then wrestle and wrestle again. Resisting conclusions that are drawn too soon. Rejecting the temptation to make deadlines on meaning-making. And slowly, bit by bit, enjoy the life-giving sense that resides at the very heart of biblical faith. Christian truths may not, finally, be quite as packagable as the philosophies offered on tomorrow's *Oprah* show.

And sometimes, if you're fortunate, you experience something that can't be photocopied or digitally processed. You discover that Xerox can't be there and that there is a mystery at the heart of God's creation—revealed to believing faith—that, even though it isn't magic, changes everything.

Consider what the book of Job, as ancient as it is, might teach about this. It's a well-known story but rather unfamiliar in its details. It may be worth careful recollection.

Here's the frame of the story. Job lived in the Land of Uz, where he was, according to Scripture, a "sound and honest" man (1:1 NJB) who "feared God and shunned evil." He had many blessings, including one wife in a time when polygamy was common. He had seven sons, three daughters, and many riches. The story calls him the "most prosperous of all the sons of the East" (1:3 NJB). He was a Bill Gates of his day, if a bit more religious. He knew all the rituals. He had the tools of faithfulness and the signs of God's favor. This Job was so faithful that when his sons would hold their customary feasts, to which they also invited their sisters—partying quite heartily, it appears—Job would go off by himself and offer the prayers and burnt offerings necessary for the spiritual protection of each child. He'd do this *just in case* they sinned, even if only in their thoughts. So this was a family man too, with all the resources and religious techniques of his day. He was ethical and dutiful before God and might have been able to get elected to the church council on a voice vote.

Now things did not remain so good for our dear Job for very long. Things fell so quickly and so dramatically, in fact, that his story stands as an allegory of inexplicable suffering. We're told that this is the great biblical text of theodicy, an attempt to interpret human pain in the face of an all-powerful God. He endured great and undeserved trials, as though caught in a battle he didn't start. Good and righteous Job became a pawn in a match between God and Satan.

Ever felt that way yourself?

God asks Satan, "Have you not seen the faithfulness of my good servant Job?"

"Oh, sure," comes Satan's cynical reply, "it's easy to believe during a bull market," reversing the old "there's no such thing as an atheist in a foxhole" theology.

"You have built a wall of protection around him in his blessings," Satan taunts. "His faith is simply thankfulness, and his devotion simply an insurance policy."

A fair enough challenge. And so indifferent to what Job or his household did or did not deserve, God allows Satan to steal Job's blessings—not only Job's flocks, herds, servants, and buildings but also his children. Satan takes everything but Job's wife and Job's health.

"And in this misfortune Job committed no sin, and he did not reproach God," the Bible says. "He kept his integrity" (1:22).

And so Satan taunts God again, claiming that as long as Job has his health he will probably stand firm. But if he were to lose that . . .

And so God, appearing to be even more arbitrary and indifferent to Job than before, allows Satan to have his way. Open sores appear over Job's body, so excessively that Job's only comfort was rolling in ashes for relief in sort of an ancient form of nonstop tar baths.

And so it goes. Understandably, Job's wife becomes embittered. And Job's friends attempt to interpret to Job his suffering and convince him he needs to repent of the sins that they are so sure are causing his ordeal.

Job's wife gives the first response. "Why persist in this integrity of yours? Why not just curse God and die?" (2:9).

Ever stoic, our dear Job actually defends God. He offers his impatient spouse a proverb of duty and forbearance. "You gotta take the good with the bad when it comes to God," he says.

And so friends Eliphaz, Bildad, and Zophar sit in silence with Job. And the tone begins to change. Exhaustion catches up with Job. He breaks to speech first and curses himself. "May the day be lost that I was born" (3:3). We would call this a death wish. We'd label him clinically depressed, if not suicidal, and get him a prescription. But his medicine is in his lament.

> My only food is sighs,
> and my groans pour out like water.
> Whatever I fear comes true,
> whatever I dread befalls me.
> For me, there is no calm, no peace;
> my torments banish rest.
>
> 3:24–26 NJB

And so now the friends take on the task of defense. Eliphaz tries to appeal to religious experience to explain Job's suffering, for Eliphaz had dreams and visions of the righteousness of those whom God corrects through pain.

Job is not convinced.

And so Bildad appeals to religious tradition, insisting that Job's suffering must be a sign of faithlessness in Job's religious practice. But Job humbly disagrees, eventually arguing with God that his suffering is, indeed, unwarranted because he had been so faithful. And Job demands an explanation from God for his difficult life.

Zophar takes the more practical approach. He is the most modern of the three. "Job, just do what you need to do to cover all the bases. It's your attitude, dude! Think positively. Say what needs to be said. Find the right way out. Please God however you have to. Just get it done! That's your best bet" (Job 11). And Job, in a long response, says to both Zophar and to God, "Leave me alone!" (Job 26–31).

Now, there's another character named Elihu in there, and much more give and take. The poetry is beautiful, and the images are often moving. But after a while, it becomes the Bible's version of a Russian novel. It's quite overwhelming to read.

And so is the point. Job exhausts himself trying to keep his control and to stay with what he thinks he knows. He pridefully asserts his innocence—challenging both his friends and God at every step—as though one tidy package would fit every problem he had.

We finally arrive at a pivotal passage some thirty-eight chapters in. All the debating with his friends comes to a close and Job stands alone before God. God then turns the tables on Job, speaking out of a tempest of power. "Now we will have a good exchange of questions," God says. "Our give and take that I will prompt will finally move us to truth."

> Where were you when I laid the earth's foundations?
> Tell me, since you are so well informed!
> Who decided its dimensions, do you know?
> Or who stretched the measuring lines across it?
> What supports its pillars at their bases?
>
> 38:4–6 NJB

And God goes on. Job interrupts, replying, in effect, "Oops! I think I've spoken too much. I seem to have angered God."

Indeed he had.

And the character of God in the melodrama speaks yet more, deepening the message that there is a power that cannot be understood. God, all powerful, is more real than Job. And Job finally relents. "I was the man who misrepresented your intentions with my ignorant words. You have told me about great works that I cannot understand, about marvels which are beyond me, of which I know nothing. . . . Before, I knew you only by hearsay but now, having seen you with my own eyes, I retract what I have said, and repent in dust and ashes" (42:3, 5–6 NJB).

Back to Job's friends. God now directs them to bring Job burnt offerings for their own repentance. Job intercedes for them. And God at long last restores Job's condition. More than that, God doubles Job's former position. Relatives and friends come to feast with him. Seven sons again, and three daughters again.

One must pity Job's wife, who apparently had to birth a least twenty babies so Job could learn his lesson and God could win this little *tête-à-tête* with Satan. But don't take the story so literally! The point here is the point. Have you ever felt so investigated by God that you were tempted to write Job's story as if it were your own?

This story is about the fact that there are some truths we cannot grasp on our own, or pin down or reproduce with ease. And it is about the fact that there is no simple *quid pro quo* in our dealings with divine reality. Talk of what one does or does not deserve never draws one closer to God. And truth cannot be designed in some perfect layout, digitized and protected in some simple and always reliable fashion as though Xerox were there. Rather than trust such facsimilies, we are called to live in awe, to know that anything may happen at any moment, to turn toward God with every effort we have, to stop grasping so hard at things or people or explanations, to give thanks, give love, and wait.

But there's another thing about Job. Look at the description of Job's life at the beginning and then at the end before you take your journey in between. See the transformation that the middle space works out. It begins in chapter 38, and its central verses are these: "Before, I knew you only by hearsay but now, having seen you with my own eyes, I retract what I have said, and repent in dust and ashes" (42:5–6 NJB). This, I believe, is the most important sentence of the book. For Job's celebrated faithfulness at the beginning of this tale, while genuine, was incomplete. Remember his isolation. His children feasted on festival days, but we are not told whether he ever joined them. We are told only that he interceded with God to protect them from judgment. There is no mention of friendships. His life is dutiful in the beginning, but—if I may stretch my point just a bit—it appears joyless when compared with the image of transformed faith at the end.

Perhaps we are to take God's praise for Job in the beginning of the story with an ever-so-slight sense of irony. For it is only at the end of the tale that we see Job feasting with his family and friends. And everything is returned to him doubly. Is this a measurable increase or one more internal, one of a mysterious *quality* of living more than an obvious *quantity* of getting?

It seems that the theological and moral correctness to which Job had so faithfully clung before has matured a bit. He is still righteous and observant, but now he is living by the spirit within the duty. And so his duty is made responsible to something outside of duty itself, something that turns his duty into joy.

Job even breaks the stricter codes of the patriarchy he once observed to now give his daughters inheritance rights, which we may take to indicate his new relationship with the law. He fulfills the law in a new way. At least one commentary on Job insists that this break with convention is merely a sign of Job's excessive wealth at the end. I doubt that conclusion. I find this act on behalf of his daughters germane to the story and essential to the twists of plot that teach us of Job's inner transformation. You see, there is no simple fixing here, no mere reproduction. There is this transformation, this doubling doubled over, doubled up, and flipped around toward God. All is new, even when it looks like it's just a return of the old.

"Before, I knew you only by hearsay but now, having seen you with my own eyes, I retract what I have said, and repent in dust and ashes." There is the power of faith.

Whether or not the outward circumstances of your life change dramatically, and whether or not you go through a dark night of the soul to get there, when you allow the distance between yourself and God to diminish, and when you resist gossip about God and search for the real thing through study, prayer, and the careful journey toward the love that would change you from the inside out, then you will know joy like Job's. The journey can be painful, but it's also lifegiving in a way no other adventure can promise.

I believe that Job's story is a story of the transformation of a soul, and we are free to suspect that while all that Job received in the end looked much like what he had in the beginning, it was, in God's grace, so much more. Thank God Xerox wasn't there.

Part 2

Sensing the World

5

Jury Duty in
the New Realm

Matthew 6:9–10

To the dismay of some of the folks I served during my years in parish ministry, I would rarely wear a clerical collar. For a funeral, I might wear one. I might wear one for particular hospital calls. And for a few other occasions, such as the administration of a sacrament, I would opt for one. These were times when I was performing a function peculiar to a pastor's ordination. But I have to think back to the late 1980s to remember when I pulled one out of my closet for any other reason. I wore a collar for a very solemn liturgical event called jury duty.

If I am ever discovered speaking or writing about the serious social responsibility Americans have to serve on juries, a duty in which I actually believe, I will likely be trying to work out my lingering shame at my early bald-faced attempt to avoid it for reasons I'm probably better off not writing about. Imagine the scene: a five-foot, eleven-inch tall, dark-haired white male in his mid-thirties sitting in a room at the federal building in downtown Chicago waiting his turn to sit in a jury pool, his collar marking a divided loyalty between church and state. His collar also marking his hope that he might be home before dinner. Lunch break came around and I still had not been called, so I walked outside and picked up a hot dog from a street vendor. I sat on a bench near one of the plazas and soon forgot about the collar.

Along walked a young man, probably about eighteen, pushing a courier's cart with boxes, apparently en route between office buildings. He slowed before approaching me, moved past, then stopped. He reversed a couple of steps, making an arc in front of me. He rested his cart against a waste can and turned in my direction.

Now if you want to experience this someday and you are not already ordained, borrow a clerical collar and spend an afternoon seeing how differently people treat you—sometimes with instant intimacy and self-disclosure, sometimes with indifference, nervousness, or unstated derision.

In this case, a somewhat jittery young man responded with self-disclosure. He asked if he might talk to me. With some hesitation I said yes, assuming he was about to ask for money to get home to Waukegan.

"Father," he said.

And then I remembered my neck. "You don't have to call me Father; I'm not a priest."

"Are you a pastor?"

"Yes."

"I need some help figuring something out. Can you help me?"

"I don't know. What's the problem?"

"I'm a Christian. Baptized about a year ago, after I found Jesus. I try real hard to live like a Christian. I praise Jesus every day, go to my church, and try to live like I should."

"Good for you! Is your church in Chicago?"

"Yeah. Here in Chicago, down south of here. I want to do what's right, what God wants me to do and all that. But I've got a problem."

"Go on, tell me more."

"Well, I've always wanted to be a policeman, you see, all my life."

"Well, that's good. Being a police officer can be a noble thing to do with your life. As long as you're honest."

"Oh, I want to be honest. No doubt about that."

"Then what's the problem?"

"Well, the elders of my church tell me that to be a good Christian I can't hurt other people; I can't kill. And they tell me that if I were in the police, I'd have to carry a gun. And if I carry a gun, I might have to use it. And if I use it, I might have to hurt someone. And if I hurt someone, I might kill them. So I don't know if I should join the police. But it's all I've ever wanted to do. So now I don't know what to do."

We discussed the matter for quite a while, me in my collar trying to get out of jury duty and he in a T-shirt struggling with faith. We discussed his motives. We discussed the need for there to be faithful people in many walks of life, and what it would be like if there were no police officers who were people of faith. And we discussed the Bible and what it means to obey God by rejecting violence and killing, and by ordering your life in a way you had never imagined before faith became real to you. We discussed his love for his church, his desire to follow the real claims his faith was making on his life, and his desire to live his life rightly. We were searching together for a treasure of insight hard to find. We parted with the question lingering. And I still hear the yearning for righteousness and truth in his voice.

It's hard being a citizen of more than one kingdom, to be marching to the beats of different drummers simultaneously. It might be easier if we could divide the two realms neatly into zones: let the church take care of my young friend's spiritual well-being, his need for care and friendship, and maybe his emotions when they get a little bit out of control, but leave the more practical things, those material, harder things to another realm and another set of experts—his schools, or the media, or the state and the way it teaches us how to be good citizens. "If the boy wants to be a policeman, what's wrong with that? The church shouldn't meddle where it doesn't belong. Let's keep things straight!"

But the prayers the church prays each time it gathers won't have that separation.

The issue for that young man was whether he should apply to the police academy, and I needed to respect that question. The issue for more of us, however, is the question for which his dilemma is a reminder, the question of these dual loyalties with which we live. When we pray the Lord's Prayer we mark our dual citizenship. We mark our split allegiance to the world in which we live and to the world beyond.

This prayer claims more territory than what we do with our private spirituality, or our emotions, or our need for good friendship. This prayer does battle with the regimes that rule our spiritual and material lives. This prayer claims our economics, our politics, our nationalities, our careers, our sexualities, our family disciplines, our finances, our relational habits and community lives, our possibilities, and our limitations. It claims *us*. The kingdom of God for which Christians pray is more than a heavenly castle; it is the entirety of the realm rendered holy, the domicile of God.

What if we were to pray instead of "Your kingdom come," something like "Your economics come," or "Your politics come," or "Your way of living come"? We'd be close to what the Bible means by the kingdom of God. The Lord's Prayer would have dealings with us in the most material and seemingly unspiritual things of our lives, and in the social order in which we live.

Don't get me wrong here. I'm not saying I believe that this boy's church was right that he shouldn't be a policeman. I'm inclined to believe he should have received different counsel. But his church was surely right in telling him that his baptism mattered and that as a citizen of two kingdoms he ought to think twice before mixing his identity with, investing his dreams in, and dedicating his moral responsibility to the authority of the kingdom of human design. That church was right in asking him to take the Lord's Prayer seriously and to make his decision with eyes wide open.

"Thy kingdom come" is, perhaps, the most dangerous passage in the Lord's Prayer. I would understand very well if those who pray the prayer hesitated before this line and withdrew their voices for fear of what these words might mean. In fact, I might be tempted to join that hesitation. But we're fortunate, in a way, that this prayer is not our own and that as we pray it we pray with Jesus, whose Spirit calls on the kingdom for us and whose Spirit tolerates our inability to understand fully what we are praying. We pray in the possibility, and maybe the hope, that these words might one day become full expressions of our hearts, even as they aren't yet today.

Tough parable, that one about the kingdom that Jesus tells in Matthew 22:1–14. The "politics of heaven" may be compared to a king who gives a wedding feast—oxen and fattened cattle slaughtered, tables groaning with food, and everything in place. He sends his servants to bring in those who had been invited to the feasting, but the servants were refused—some were battered and some were killed. Now, this was no gentle invitation. Nor was it politely refused because of the demands of busy schedules. Read Matthew's version of this story. He pulls no punches.

In the ancient Near East, when you were summoned to a feast thrown by a king you went. You have received that kind of invitation, one that you know you cannot turn down. Maybe your job required it. Or maybe networks of obligations and choices you've made in your life committed you. Or maybe it simply involved one of those friendships that become joyful obligations. "We need you!" And you go. And woe to you if you don't, for if you don't, you lose a bit of your capacity for commitment and you lose a bit of yourself.

The kingdom of God summons us a bit like that. And part of the adventure of faith is learning how to order your life so that you can accept the invitation to such heavenly feasting and discover purposes for your days that resemble God's love for the world.

So please understand one thing about praying for the coming of the kingdom of God: you are joining Jesus and his followers throughout the ages in doing more than simply acknowledging such a radical demand on your life. You are actually seeking this demand. You are praying for the Sovereign's party to commence, and you are placing yourself on the invitation list for reasons you may spend your life sorting out. There's a sloppiness to the life of saints, you see, because they are often dropping their plans and rearranging things in the moment when glimpses of the new realm appear.

Our citizenship in the world is not nearly so serious as we are led to believe—what we do, who we do it with, how we look, how safe and secure we are, how much power we've accumulated or confidence in the future we've achieved. It's not so serious because at any moment we may find ourselves on a different invitation list. What is more serious is how we order our living in the world so that we can recognize the invitation when it's offered. To pray "Thy kingdom come" is to say that you want to learn how to hold life like an eggshell, very lightly, trusting that right under the surface, if you let Christ's Spirit break through, is a richer and deeper and fuller realm.

Consider a little fantasy story by C. S. Lewis called *The Great Divorce*. A group of souls in hell take a bus ride to heaven to check things out and explore whether they'd rather be there than in hell. Getting off the bus, they move onto a beautiful, dew-covered lawn only to discover the grass won't bend under their feet. Imagine blades so sharp you're afraid to touch them. Imagine strength like diamonds. Small leaves as heavy as a load of coal. Not even the dew drops are disturbed.[1] All was too real. Even the simplest things were so real they were dangerous.

So real is the realm of God. No quaint theological discussion groups. Just reality. Like yeast that cannot be seen but is the reality of the bread. Like buried treasure making the field more valuable than anyone can imagine. Like a pearl of great price or a seed that disappears into a growing plant. The kingdom of God is that hidden realm that, when you open yourself to it, re-creates, enlivens, and humbles the world we've created.

This kingdom, this economics, this politics, is here and not here. And this quality of being present and absent is the push and pull quality of biblical existence. It is a quality of yearning that sits right in the heart of faith. We yearn for perfection, for completion, for a home far away, and find that yearning taking us right back into the home we make here.

I once heard of a rabbi who says that if you don't weep just a little at the end of each day, tears of both sorrow and joy, you may not know faith. We love each other, and love the world, because we know that there is more. Figure that one out, and live in the freedom that insight gives. You can face yourself honestly, and approach the world fearlessly, because you know that there is a hidden reality both in your soul and in the world, and that this reality is God's.

This knowledge gives both peace, because we know we needn't control the future, and restlessness, because we know things are not yet well. This peaceful restlessness leans us forward, up on the tips of our toes, to see what God is bringing to birth. We are created for no better purpose than to watch expectantly, live accordingly, worship happily, and serve gratefully in anticipation of God's kingdom.

Throughout the New Testament, something is always just about to happen. And that is the sense that fills the prayer "Your kingdom come." The life-changing challenges of dual citizenship are laid bare. And I believe there lies the richest living of all. And if my young friend at that plaza in Chicago teaches anything, I hope he keeps teaching this.

6

Ringmaster Ned

Matthew 21:1–15

Peanuts . . . popcorn . . . peanuts . . . popcorn . . ." It was one
of those events in a teenager's life that passes not fully ap-
preciated until the images and sensations come back one day
in adulthood. I think the scientific term is *learning experience*.

At sixteen years old, not fearless by nature, I was a little nervous. A tray with a strap to go over my neck was thrust into my
hands. There was a construction worker's apron inside. I was
told to tie it around my waist to collect the money. And to clip
on my belt there was one of those metal clicker coin holders for
making change.

Buddy or Bruno or Buster or whatever the name was of the
"been round the bend a few times" roadie who gave us our five
minutes' worth of instructions had a voice that grumbled like a

rough morning after a few too many cigarettes. "Popcorn's fifty cents. Peanuts are seventy-five. When you run out, come down, get refilled, and be sure to empty the money. No foolin' around. You're here to work. Don't watch the show. Shout over the crowd so people know what you're selling. And if you're carrying Pepsi, don't spill it or we'll charge you! Now count off: number 1, you get section A; number 2, section B; number 3, C; and so on. Got it? I want you selling as soon as you hit the stands. If you haven't sold out at least once before the parade begins, you're doing something wrong. Move the merchandise!"

He disappeared. We laughed in anticipation, made adolescent jokes, acted like everything was cool when we were actually more giddy than confident and more scared than in command. A few minutes later, I was walking up and down section F of the grand Exhibition Hall at the Michigan State Fair Grounds in Detroit hawking my wares at the Annual Shrine Circus as part of a charity fund-raiser.

"Peanuts . . . popcorn . . ." I said timidly. "Peanuts . . . popcorn . . ." I said a bit more confidently. "Peanuts . . . popcorn . . ." I finally found my voice. "Seventy-five cents, sir. That'll be fifty cents, ma'am." I did sneak up to the top under the girders a couple of times, just to take in the scene. And it was something to behold. Three large rings below, just high enough off the ground to mark protected space, yet low enough to keep spectators' hearts racing with the thought that something might spill over into the stands at any moment. Activity everywhere. Each ring working. Smell of sawdust. Sound of a circus organ over a crackly public address system and the voice of the top-hatted ringmaster. The whole world passing before our eyes. Adults sat remembering their youth and occasionally letting go to enjoy. Children with their eyes wide open not knowing what to look at next, gasping at just the moments the ringmaster wanted them to. And older kids looking down and around trying to figure out where they fit, acting more aloof than they really were.

In the center ring were tightrope walkers and trapeze artists. Inside the left ring were the exotic but seemingly docile animals, named and dolled up with ruffles and hats for their fans. That extra-long whip snapped to the ground as a signal for the old elephant Molly to put her foot on top of the barrel and bounce a ball on her trunk. And of course, the dancing bears. And in the opposite ring, the human cannonball and other such feats of daring. Fire eaters and those rope swingers—I don't remember what they're called. And the clowns everywhere, jumping into barrels of water between acts or bopping each other over the head with giant hammers just before the lion tamers came out. Now they, the lion tamers, got the center ring with the others emptied out. They displayed their fiercest of beasts, each on the edge of wild—nature conforming to human power, daring danger, human dexterity and extraordinary skill.

Violence and wonder, smells and bells, kitsch and nonsense. Space and time marked off, with peanuts and popcorn to boot. All for a few bucks, and profits to charity. Not a bad evening out.

Even if you've never witnessed an old fashioned three-ring circus, you may yet nod when you think of circuslike life experiences. I recommend that tray of popcorn around your neck and change-clicker on your belt. They give their own perspective. They help you feel like you're part of the show, like Ringmaster Ned directing our attention in the midst of the hubbub. Or like Bozo the Clown, hired to distract our attention, make us laugh, and remind us that the familiar can coexist with the bizarre. Or like the owner of the donkey who gave the ride that led the Greatest Entrance of All Time.

Reading the stories of Holy Week feels a bit like that night, with life experience our section F. The Circus of All the World before us, come into town from Bethpage near Bethany, here for one and all. And we're looking down through the rows at it all.

"In the red, white, and blue ring," our ringmaster barks, "we have the family of performers called politics—and economics too." Circus artists indeed. Consider the show in any given week: cycles of vengeance and retribution harming hopes for peace, one

region or another on the brink, quiet and not so quiet despera-
tion all about. And the list of feats gets long. There's a bread line
in one part of the ring. And yet others come in dressed up and
doing well. There's some peace over here, and even something
like democracy springing up over there—just enough to keep us
ooing and ahhing. Amazing what can fit inside such a space.

And to your left, in the purple ring of this metaphor, we are
presented religion. This is a show set for all to see—the greatest on
earth, to be sure. It's circus at its best, and worst. A great liturgy
is being acted out, moving and deep for many, comic for some,
and simply a convenient place to hide for others. There's anger
erupting over differences in one place. The authorities are clamp-
ing down and closing it down in others; "In the best interests of
the community," says the sign they carry. A bit of a show trial is
going on in another place, with the players on both sides acting
so sure of themselves. Circuses are always bigger than life. And
here and there folks are being baptized, are praying and loving,
grieving over losses and grateful for blessings, touching a light
shining through the big top and looking at their hands inside its
beam, and breaking the rules by stepping over the ring to take
gifts to folks in the audience. That's religion for you. Amazing
what can fit inside such a space.

And in the center ring, with the golden paint, is the future—the
future of truth, of flesh and spirit, of the lives we're living, of all
people and all time, and of creation itself. So goes the show into
which Jesus comes.

If we lay the three rings over the story of that fateful Sunday
before Christ was crucified, the Sunday Christians call Palm Sunday, the center ring will circle the temple and all that happens
there, from the overturned tables outside to the veil that is torn
apart inside. The cage opens for the tiger to roam, tamed and
wild at the same time.

And like all good circuses, this one too begins with a parade,
just on the other side of the Mount of Olives. All the animals in

their cars, the jugglers walking alongside, tumblers somersaulting, midgets and lepers, folks who'd been miraculously healed: the man born blind, watch him count the fingers on your hand; or meet Lazarus, still smelling of burial spice, walking and talking and praising God.

And like every good parade, this one brings some unplanned action. Folks gather along the road, hearing rumors that the Galilean is heading toward Jerusalem. From a reasonable distance, it looks like they are supporters. They find the leader strangely seated on a donkey. And they become a part of it all by breaking branches off of trees to line the road and laying their cloaks on top of the palms for Jesus to ride on.

They begin to shout, "Hosanna!" The word means far more than "welcome" or "glory." It's an appeal. "Hear us! Look positively upon us! Favor us! Favor us, O Favored One, all the way to the highest heaven!" Here is a blending of religion and politics into something quite remarkable. And for those who have a sense for what's happening, it's much more than just circus, even when that's all it looks like.

A few steps farther back and you get a broader view. As the parade circles and comes closer, you notice that some of the politicians and priests are gathering in their own bunches, fingers wagging, jittery, angry, perspiring a little too much. Never joined the parade, actually, so never laid down their own cloaks.

That one on the donkey dismounts and steps over the two-foot barrier ringing the sacred grounds and gives an unforgettable performance. Even while other things are going on, all eyes are on Jesus. And that's precisely the problem as far as the skeptical ones are concerned. For no one, not even a prophet of God, should receive that much attention, they think. Threatens business, you see. Undermines authority. Messes up the show.

But it can't be stopped, and so the drama takes another turn. You'll hear hisses at the evil characters hell-bent from the start to grab hold of the microphone and call the shots. And you'll catch oohs and uh-ohs at the more well-meaning players dressed up like public officials and spiritual leaders, waffling, blundering, and becoming tools of the great God-destruction. And at some point you'll sense even the hosanna crowd shifting its affections. Maybe then, when it all begins to unfold, it would be a good time to sit down on those sticky cement steps, popcorn tray on your lap, and try to sort it out.

For you see, in between all the other things going on, God is actually securing the future. God's stealing the show, for those with eyes to spot it. Spy those intimate scenes played out here and there: around the table in the Upper Room, in the garden of Gethsemane, by the fire and in the court of King Herod, on the death walk to Golgotha, at the foot of the cross—each as revealing of this miracle-working, parade-leader Jesus-God as any event of his ministry. And follow the sad clown Judas, perhaps the saddest of all, if you know the story, who dons his face to play his part, laughs in a way larger than life, weeps to the point of his own demise, and loses himself in a story he tries to control but never can.

On that side, crucifixion. On this side, the ringmaster still trying to move your attention elsewhere. You may still be looking at the other performances and you just don't see what I'm describing in the center, whether because of unanswered questions, or hurt, or fear. But you keep looking.

It would be easier if everything just stopped when Jesus rode in, if all the buzz quieted and all good hearts listened up. But that doesn't seem to be the way this God, known in Christ Jesus, is revealed. This God is more gracious and finally more creative than that. For fear of belaboring the point, it's just a whole lot more like a circus than that. Everything is happening all the time, even as God speaks, and even as Jesus lives, and even as the Spirit moves among the rings. This God comes like events unfold in Holy Week, through decisions and sorrow as well as acceptance and gratitude, and through suffering and political frustration as well as through liberation and good works.

If you are distracted by the Spirit's modesty and wish it all were simpler and grander with only one voice controlling the hubbub, this picture of the world may not satisfy. Your voice is one of

those that want to bring order to the busyness. That's fine. May
you shout for joy and argue for a way that brings peace to the
chaos. Please argue well, though. Woo, give witness, and model
the way of peace you would urge others to follow. Don't impose,
for the circus can turn ugly when the choreography that makes
it a spectacle is overwhelmed by just one act. There's reason to
believe that God graces us with freedom not because there is no
better way than the chaos freedom brings, but in order to preserve
enough diversity in life that we can keep violence to a minimum
while we await the day of lasting unity.

And if you are too preoccupied with cares and concerns to stop
and look again at what God might be doing in the world, there's
no easy answer for you either. For there are times when the tasks
of life simply overwhelm the attention required to see God at
work. May you, in your days, find your burden lifted—whether
by a neighbor's hand offering help or by a spiritual hand offering
strength—long enough for you to say, "Yes, yes, I remember; the
day *is* holy, and all time *is* God's."

And you may know the stories of faith so well and love them
so much that you want to get to the finale as soon as possible.
The promise of Easter is rich indeed. For you, Christ's wish may
be simple. May your confidence in the real joy that awaits be so
strong that you can rest and watch and see new opportunities to
live out your faith around you. And maybe you will be the one
who reaches out to help or encourage the ones who are burdened
or distracted. And maybe you will be the one who keeps the peace
without doing harm.

This circus illustration breaks down in the end. And rightly so.
For the events that make up the life of Jesus and the polyphony of
the world he came to save outstrip any analogy or hook anyone
might use to give them meaning. Perhaps that's why I write of
that memory of a circus in the first place. Not because it says anything helpful in itself about this God and these days but because
it just feels more like the life into which Jesus comes than some
of the more coherent descriptions of living available. And it feels
more like the world in which and for which God dies, and for

which and into which God is raised. All the political, religious, and personal intrigues of the moment are on display. Waiting to be overturned, redeemed, and made whole.

It's the Greatest Show of All, and it's God's.

7

9/12 Living in a 9/11 World

Luke 18:1–8

Not long after September 11, 2001, the *Washington Post* ran an article by Hanna Rosin titled "In Terror's Wake: 'God, You Around?'" It was about the resurgence of both outward religious practice and private prayer in the wake of that September's events. "It's not just that the faithful are flocking to houses of worship," she wrote, "it's that people who have never been and still won't go, who passed all those candlelight vigils . . . and kept on walking, are finding themselves, despite themselves, praying." She quotes the head of a network of counselors working mostly with New York business folk: "'Every other person we spoke to would get to a point where they'd say, "Doc, I'm not sleeping well and the only way I can get through this is to pray."'" And she describes a graffiti artist who once "peppered the sidewalks with, 'No more prisons,'" but had taken to writing, simply, "Pray."[1]

To feel secure. To feel whole. To find eternity in the midst of a world that feels uncontrollable, contingent, and pretty chancy. To see grievances redressed. To find justice. "Where the corpse is, there the vultures will gather," Jesus says (Matt. 24:28 NJB). A nicer way of saying that might be, "Hey! Read the signs."

There are times, are there not, when despite all you do to nail life down, you sense you still need something you can't perfectly name or easily control? You look up and away, as if to distract your attention from whatever's going on just long enough to let that something well up inside and give you a little more confidence or a little more hope or a few more reasons to believe that things will be okay. It's not just about those odd weeks in October 2001. It's about more ordinary times too.

"Lord, increase our faith!" shouted strongly, as a plea.

"Lord . . . increase our faith," whispered hesitantly, as a hope.

There is a patch of Scripture that ends with a story about a widow and a judge (Luke 18). This patch begins when the closest followers of Jesus face him with their growing unease. The new life they had chosen with him was feeding fears of what the future might demand: "Lord, increase our faith!" And Christ's response: "If you had faith the size of a mustard seed, you could say to the Washington Monument, 'Jump up in the air and fly over the city, spin around the House of Representatives, then go off and drop into the Potomac,' and you know, it would." Faith that small can do that much.

Ever hold a mustard seed? It's tiny. Its size might lead one to conclude that Jesus is suggesting the apostles' pleading for a value-added kind of believing is just slightly misplaced. For faith the size of a mustard seed isn't much faith, and so we can conclude that it doesn't take much faith or much trust or much of the stuff that we spend so much time on in the church to get some power going. I mean, a mustard seed can levitate a tree without even using a trowel, Jesus says.

Now, if at the start of this little exchange their faith was smaller than that seed, we are to surmise either that these followers of Jesus had nearly no faith at all or that what they're calling faith is just not quite what Jesus wants for them. They're obsessed with something rather beside the point. For it takes hardly any of what they're looking for to give you the illusion of control. The more precious thing, the truer thing that takes us toward God, might look a little different than the kind of faith we use to simply add value to lives more quickly based on other dreams.

Consider the story about the disciples coming to Jesus, nervous about how they were going to pay their taxes (Matt. 17:24–27). Jesus sends them down to the river to fish. "The first fish you catch will have a silver coin in its mouth. Pay the taxes with that." Might sound a bit flippant, like Jesus is telling them to be reckless. But it might also be something else. It may be a lesson about staying passionate about the things God is passionate about and not confusing God's cares with the cares and concerns handed us by more worldly affairs.

Remember the ten lepers who cry out to Jesus for mercy (Luke 17:12–19). Jesus sends them to the priests to fulfill their religious duty. "Be purified before seeking your healing," Jesus says. And they're healed before they even reach the temple door. Just turning and moving was seed enough to heal their bodies. But when only one among the ten—and the foreign one, a Samaritan at that—comes back to thank Jesus, Jesus says, "You! Your faith has grown by your courage to see through your experience to its source, and by your courage to say thank you. That faith has made you more than healthy. It has made you well. Go and live."

So here's a reasonable conclusion: you have enough faith. Simple as that. You don't have to keep fighting. You can pause, and you can watch, and you can wait to spy what God might be doing in the world without worrying about yourself. And you are free to care more about God than what the rest of us seem to be busying ourselves with. And you're free to look for other folks who've spied this too. Stop fretting about faith, and start exploring God.

Oh, but the story about that Samaritan has another twist. Seems the church council happened by to see Jesus after it happened. "Yes, yes, healing and all that. But we're trying to work out an appropriate budget versus pledge algebra in the wake of current economic uncertainty, and so would appreciate some sense of when the reign of God will begin full-fledged. We may want to borrow against that inside knowledge." Or in a better translation, "When is the kingdom of God coming?" And Jesus, once again, answers awry, "The kingdom of God is not coming by things that can be observed. ('To the left, there it is!' Or, 'To the right, *there* it is!') No, no, no!"

Consider the prospect: the folks are finally doing okay and the children are well. The house is refinanced. The application for college admission or a new job is in the mail, and you feel good about your chances. You know who you are and what you're doing, maybe for the first time ever. We're feeling secure. We can go back to putting "No more prisons" on the sidewalks. Ordinary life can be okay. The Jesus of Scripture does not despise it. But I do think this about what Jesus says to the church council: you can't read the New Testament without coming to the conclusion that God sees even more than we, that even in an ordinary life anything can happen at any moment. Contingency is the most we can predict. A phone call, a letter, an incoming something that becomes news, *real* news. And you discover that living an ordinary life does not equal living a secure or predictable life.

"Lying in bed, finally happy, and one of you is taken," Scripture imagines (Luke 17:33). "Doing your duty, grinding that meal, and it all stops suddenly" (v. 35). And Jesus says, without guile, "Those who try to make their life secure will lose it, but those who lose their life will keep it" (Luke 17:33 NRSV). And what are we to do with that? "Pray always and don't lose heart," comes the reply.

God's reign, like God's presence in our lives, is as elusive and hard to fathom as it is so present it fills the air. It is like the flash lightning that comes as if from nowhere. Night becomes day in an instant. You can see the storm, but you can't predict the lightning. "It's like day in the middle of the night," I heard a child say of such a flash. And it can be as scary as it is attractive.

It seems that in a certain city there was a judge who "neither feared God nor had respect for people" (Luke 18:2 NRSV). Not a great recommendation. And in this city lived someone rather like that Samaritan who was healed and came back to thank Jesus. She was a widow, which in Jesus' day meant that she was left quite alone and vulnerable. We can assume that she had no economic, judicial, social, or even family status except what was given her by the good will of those who were better off.

Now, this widow experienced an injustice for which she justly deserved redress. But she knew, as do you and I, that the offices of the world can prove awfully indifferent. "Too many demands and too few resources," we're told. "That approach doesn't fit protocol." "We can't approve that program because we've got to pay for the war." Competition is no friend to the needy, and our widow knows this better than most (Luke 18:1–8).

The text tells us that this judge thought to himself, "I really don't care about this poor widow's grievance and don't think it makes any claim on me at all. But she keeps bothering me. I just want her to go away!" Squeaky wheel gets the oil. "I don't want her to wear me out!" he says. An accurate translation here would read, "I don't want her to blacken my eye," much like saying of a politician sullied by scandal that she "got a black eye from the press." While the woman was screaming, "Hey, everybody, you seem to think this judge is so fair. Look what he's doing to me!" our judge kept muttering to himself, "Don't want scandal. Must keep my reputation intact. I'll give her what she wants to shut her up." We used to call it hush money. This widow knew whom to trust and whom not to trust. She also knew how to get what she needed.

"Pay close attention to this judge," Jesus says. Remember that just because the widow got what she needed, we should not conclude that the world is just. Work the world for good, to benefit the most vulnerable. Find mercy where you can find it. But don't trust the world. Just don't trust it. Trust God. Pray to God. Trust not the judge. Pray not to the judge.

And here we come back to that October in 2001 when, by all appearances, all sorts of folk were going to church. The world was no less dangerous or chancy on September 10 of that year than it was the day Hanna Rosin's article appeared. For we know, when we dare to admit it, that all can be well and all can fall apart at any moment of any day in any month of any year. And I believe the truth is also this: God chooses this widow, and that Samaritan, and the other street painter, with the truest of all compassion. And God makes a promise to do justice—as long as we don't trust our own measure or our own justice too much. For God's eye is not blackened, and we need not nag.

Might this apply beyond our own lives, to the world outside us? Here's one way to consider that question. Ubiquitous flag-waving and indecorous displays of congressmen courting votes by grandstanding the Pledge of Allegiance on the Capitol steps may imitate the judge of this parable sooner than the victim. For the God whose promise is deeper, broader, and finally more just than the fragile dreams of national pride spreads divine compassion from Palestine in Ohio to Palestine in the Middle East. This God does not value one over the other, except where people suffer want and injustice. And this is a God who would call out of us a seed-sized faith that bridges that divide in a way our politics cannot imagine. Flag waving that leads to fearless effort on behalf of *all* victims is worthy of New Testament faith. Flag waving that signals defiance and threat is another thing altogether.

"Increase our faith!" Demand this with sincere desire. But be sure the faith you want increased is not depleted of the very faith Jesus would have for you. For the faith Christ seeks, at least as the Scriptures seem to teach it, is a faith born of trust *beyond* the intrigues of the world. It is a faith that can take contingency and chance, savvy and persistence, small gratitudes for blessings unexpected, and mustard-seed-sized confidence and transform these things into a hope that breaks through all the fear. And this is a faith that finally cries to God from the chastened and awakened depths of our spirits when facing the world honestly: "God! God! Help us see, help us hear, help us live a faith that wraps in your compassion and mercy all that you have chosen—in every place and in every time, widows and judges together. Samaritans and compatriots. All."

To feel secure. To feel whole. To find eternity in the midst of a world that feels uncontrollable, contingent, pretty chancy. To see grievances redressed. To find justice.

Read the signs.

8

No Wilder Peace

Isaiah 10:33–11:10
and Matthew 3:1–12

He left California for Israel in 1968 to make his return, or his *aliyah*. His army service began three years later, right after graduating from high school. He cherished his Zionist dreams and was confident of the righteousness of his cause, and he was sure he knew the story. He also had a heart of compassion, an unusual openness, and a relentless desire to root truth in both honesty and hopefulness. He took his rabbinical studies in the U.S. and then returned in 1981 just after being ordained as a rabbi in the Conservative movement. And then Israel invaded Lebanon. It wasn't long before he began to see and hear more than he thought he knew, and his sense of the world began to shift.

I met Jeremy two years after that invasion, and that's when he told me his story. Not because he saw it as heroic; telling it was just a part of conversation between new friends describing bits and pieces of their lives.[1]

He was called up to serve in the military and went to Lebanon with the others. It wasn't long before he found he couldn't eat. Didn't really know why, but he knew he just couldn't eat. Concern moved up the ranks. He was told the food was kosher and that he should have no problem eating. He was also reminded of his religious responsibility, as a clergyman, to set a good example. But he couldn't eat. This went on for a bit. No explanation. He didn't really know the reason himself, just something welling up inside.

He was told again, and then again, that the food was prepared properly and there was no religious reason why he shouldn't eat. Eventually the reason came, and overflowed. He discovered it as he told it. "I know how the food is prepared, and that causes me no concern. It is not the preparation. For no matter how the food is prepared, if it is served here it is not kosher."

Jeremy was quickly sent home to a desk job. Setting an example. At home he became one of the founding members of Yesh Gvul, an organization of Israeli soldiers who first refused to serve in Lebanon and later, even until now, refuse to serve in the Palestinian territories. Yesh Gvul also defends Israelis who seek to refuse military service altogether, even though there is no recognized conscientious-objector status in Israel.

I have no right, nor desire, to make a claim about what is or is not kosher in a Jewish sense. I only mean to give witness to this one man's testimony.

I met Jeremy in a seminar on pacifism and nonviolence at an Inter-Faith Institute near Bethlehem. On the afternoon he told me of his experience in Lebanon he also said that if anyone had told him ten years before that he'd be sitting and learning, working and demonstrating, walking and eating, and feeling such kinship with more Christians and Muslims in Israel than he had in California, he'd have laughed. But here he was.

He told me about visiting a Palestinian Muslim village and finding himself caught near Sabbath sundown in the midst of a demonstration against military expropriation of land and the government's refusal to provide basic services. He had to choose between competing obligations. That evening he found a way. He stayed for the demonstration and spent his Sabbath nightfall as a guest in the home of a Muslim family. They prepared a Sabbath meal for him the best they could, in hospitality and in friendship.

I asked Jeremy once if as a result of all the adjustments and compromises he has made to keep doing the work he does, he feels less religious. "No," he responded. "I feel more."

"They shall not hurt nor destroy on all my holy mountain," says the Lord (Isa. 65:25 NRSV).

But Jeremy Milgrom is not the topic of this writing. The tenth chapter of Isaiah is, and what Isaiah the prophet saw: shoots from stumps, branches from roots, a little child, a holy mountain, and a banner that will draw all nations to itself. This writing is about how God might be working—then and now.

The poem of Isaiah 10 and 11 is a classic pre-Christmas Scripture, read year after year in early Advent, except that the Advent reading is usually begun a few verses later than where it should be, probably to avoid the images of destruction that begin the poem. Such images are not so good for Christmas, so the Advent passage is usually begun with the image of a shoot sprouting from Jesse's stump: "And there shall come forth a rod out of the stem of Jesse, and a Branch shall grow out of his roots. And the spirit of the Lord shall rest upon him" (Isa. 11:1, 2a KJV). It is traditionally associated with Romans 15, where Paul writes that out of the root of Jesse will come one to rule over the Gentiles. So Isaiah, too, is taken to be saying that a messiah will come from Jesse's lineage. This is the lineage of old Israel's King David, which is also the lineage of Jesus. It works especially well at Christmastime because the passage ends up talking about a little child leading the people to a world of peace. But if you start at the poem's beginning and resist the Christmas spirit for a moment, a more syncopated beat comes up.

The passage comes up in the midst of a passionate account of God's judgment on history. The judgment is first on God's own people for their unfaithfulness and their injustice: "For iniquitous decrees, and oppressive laws, for refusing justice to the needy, and rights to the poor" (Isa. 10:1–2 NRSV). In response, God has taken away the kingdom, using Assyria as a weapon to do this.

After a long time away from home and in an unusual moment of national penitence Isaiah finally hears God reassuring these people in exile, that though Assyria has been used to mete out this judgment, God will eventually turn divine attention toward Assyria as well. For no people escape God's judgment. And so the time is coming when divine wrath will return, though then against Assyria (10:24–26). When this happens, a remnant of God's people will be restored to their former place and the reign of justice will once again be described and may finally commence. Isaiah imagines this wrath: "The Lord will lop the boughs off trees, leaving only stumps. The Lord will bring the lofty low, and will hack the majestic cedar forests of Lebanon with an axe. The trees will fall, leaving heaves of roots. And the stumps and roots intertwine" (10:33–34). The forests of Assyria and Lebanon will all be stubble, like Israel has been all along—power leveled as empire crumbles. And so we arrive at the edge of a long drawn-out metaphor about roots and branches.

Here's the first move of the metaphor: measure the devastation, even the uprooting of the pecking order that the weak know so well. Measure the laying low of the woods so great. Measure it, see it, and describe it. Then a second move: break the rod with which you've measured the devastation, just as God breaks the rod of divine judgment.

The stump of ancient Israel, the so-called stump of Jesse, gets all wrapped up with what Isaiah sees God doing with *everyone*. And from this devastation, this stump, Isaiah sees that something will sprout. The Spirit of the Lord will rest on Jesse and change him into wisdom, counsel, might, knowledge, and fear of God—with all of this turned into divine delight. A new kind of judgment will be meted out. Israel will no longer resign itself to inequity. No longer bound to cowardly vision:

"Oh, that's just the way of the world."

"No one to negotiate with, after all."

"Our hands are tied."

"Collateral damage."

"Pity the poor or those who just happen to be in the wrong place at the wrong time. Too bad they weren't born somewhere else. Too bad they can't just move out of the way. But they made their bed . . ."

Isaiah will have none of this. For this new people will judge not by what seems to be the inevitable, even if tragic, case. This Jesse will not decide by what he hears in the hallways or coffee shops. He will judge rightly and, at long last, fairly. He will judge the way the better angels of our conscience imagined judgment all along: for the meek, for the poor, for the ones who just can't get out of the way in time.

So consider a clergyman named for the prophet Elijah, Elias in Arabic. He is a Palestinian Melkite priest, Father Elias Chacour. He is called Abuna ("Daddy") by those who honor his ministry. For thirty years Abuna Chacour has been working in his own way for justice, reconciliation, and compassionate education for Israelis and Palestinians. In a little village in Galilee he built an elementary school, then a high school, and now a college. His goal is to attract Palestinians in the diaspora to return to teach at the college. And he dreams of unprecedented permission from the Israelis to teach Jews as well as Arabs in his schools. On the grounds of Mar Elias College stands a memorial for the Holocaust called "The Listening Post." It is two curved walls, which if linked would form a perfect circle. On one side there is written in

Arabic, "Memorial to the Jewish Martyrs." On the other side, in Hebrew, "Memorial to the Palestinian Martyrs." Abuna Chacour has written about the message of this memorial:

> It is insane to continue with the satanic method: reaction—reaction; violence for violence, teeth for one tooth . . . it is time that we introduce the freedom of the One hanging on the cross, I mean our Compatriot, Jesus from Nazareth. The ultimate expression of freedom was expressed while He was hanging on the cross: "Father forgive them, they do not know what they do."[2]

I sat with Abuna on his roof one hot August night in 1982. Israeli warplanes could be heard overhead on their way to bomb Beirut. Jeremy may still have been up there, hungry, for all I know. The night was as dark as a small village with no streetlights can be. And the despair of this priest was as deep as that darkness.

It was the night of the Feast of Elijah, the annual celebration of Abuna Chacour's patron saint. But there was no comforting this Elias as he spoke with unusual candor and the pain only a full and open heart can bear. Perhaps he was most honest with us, as we were five ministry students from a land not his own.

As we sat in long silences broken only by the sounds of the jets and his lament, one of the nuns rushed up the stairs.

"Abuna, Abuna!" she said. "Look, look to the school."

We rose together, fearful of seeing harm. We looked over the cemented stone wall of the flat roof. We peered through the night across the valley that separated the rectory from the shell of the high school building being constructed on the top of the next hill. The school children had taken luminaries and placed one in the shell of each room and dozens in a shepherding circle at the base of the whole structure, all in honor of the Feast of Elijah and in loving thanks to their Father. And tears came. Something, again, about holy mountains, lambs living with wolves, leopards lying down with kids.[3]

> The nursing child shall play over the hole of the asp,
> and the weaned child shall put its hand on the adder's den.

They will not hurt or destroy
on all my holy mountain;
for the earth will be full of the knowledge of the LORD
as the waters cover the sea.
On that day the root of Jesse shall stand as a [luminary] to the
    peoples.

ISAIAH 11:8–10 NRSV

And the Christian Peacemaker Teams continue their work, with one of their most volatile projects centered in the West Bank town of Hebron. The work began as a mediating witness to the work of nonviolence and a testimony to the possibility of reconciliation against all odds. They wear red cloaks. They pray, train, and ready themselves to move into confrontations, often placing themselves between soldiers and demonstrators in hopes of preventing violence in either direction. They surround houses so American-built Caterpillar bulldozers driven by confused operators can't demolish homes for the convenience of Israeli settlers, or for the building of what's been called a "security" wall, or in collective punishment.

These are ordinary folk. They're just as nervous as anyone, just as worried, just as ambitious, just as mixed up and mixed in, just as loving, just as hopeful for an ordinary and satisfying life. And they want an ordinary life for others too. But they find themselves following God to Hebron.

The organization decided to ignore American government recommendations about leaving the occupied territories. They decided to continue in their work, as best they could, against the tide of history. And they decided to bind themselves to a new branch. You see, they believe that the branch really is growing, even now, from upturned roots of devastation. Metaphor becoming fact.

By the summer of 2002, the Hebron team had already three times issued a statement saying that even as they are committed to taking the risks required for their witness, they do not believe that others should be forced to take risks to save them. And so to live this conviction with integrity and avoid any harm that might contradict the better part of their intention, they asked that if they are ever in such danger that bystanders, rescuers, or anyone involved needs to take undue risk to save them, no such risk be taken. They are willing to die.

Yet neither Elias Chacour nor the Christian Peacemaker Teams are the topic of this writing either. Isaiah is, and along with him John the Baptizer and John's message in the wilderness to "Repent, for the kingdom of heaven has come near."

The account of John in the Gospel of Matthew relates to Isaiah's vision of Jesse. Consider what Matthew suggests about John's attitude toward the religious elite. John calls them a brood of vipers and tells them that having a noble ancestry and impeccable credentials means nothing. Only people whose lives are worthy of repentance could come to be baptized by John, not the corrupted religious and political leaders. In effect, he warned them that God was cutting the forest again.

I find the story Matthew's gospel tells of John's refusing to baptize the religious and political leaders disturbing, because as Matthew tells it one can't help but get the impression that these leaders were not coming to taunt John at all. Nor were they coming to trap him or undermine his message. It seems, at least as Matthew tells it, that they were actually coming to be baptized. And yet John still turns them away. Why? I'm left wondering if even as they were coming to be baptized, they may yet have been claiming pride of place against the poorer folk waiting. Perhaps they did this by claiming their status and authority, and the privilege of power. Perhaps they leveraged this into advantage as they elbowed their way to the front of the line, or protected themselves from the hot sun with canopies brought from the city while folks from the countryside burned. Perhaps John was simply calling them on their presumption.

Hard to know. But it does appear that when standing before the witness of Jeremy, Elias, the Christian Peacemaker Teams, Isaiah's vision, and John's call, I have no special permission to let go or push in or give up because I may be Christian or American or educated or secure or anything else I might use to shield myself from the pain of others. I may be something or have something that leaves me less able to know that God is the God of all people, and that God can work divine purpose in the midst of the most disturbing devastation, and that God desires a compassionate order judged by something other than what we normally see or hear.

Though the boughs are being cut down and the roots are being upended, hope remains a branch. And hope remains the holy mountain up which the vulnerable child who breaks the rod of violence will lead those who will follow. And hope remains the Promised One.

You'll know it in your spirit, in the truthfulness, the peace, and the better hope you finally say yes to in the midst of more ordinary stuff. And you'll know it among the people, in the basic decency and fair dealings for which the church continues to dream. And you'll begin to see it out and about in the world in testimonies of quiet courage, in the rocklike witness to works of love that are free of cynicism, in freedom that is free of tyranny, in meetings between enemies free of violence, and in voices that don't mock God. And we can see it in the little child for whom we wait and in whom we find power enough to measure, un-measure, and unmeasure our unmeasuring in turn, so to begin to see the world remade.

From such a stump as this comes such a branch.

Part 3

Sensing the Church

9

Blinded by the Light

Mark 9:2–8

From one perspective, this thing we call Christianity is an elaborate prescription for spiritual frustration. It is as though Christian talk of religious experience and the truth of God in our lives merely sets us up for failures and broken promises. Those failures begin with somewhat dysfunctional delivery systems, whether the Old Testament people of Israel or the New Testament church. Vessels said to contain the pure stuff of God seem so full of cracks that the very thing they are designed to bear leaks through, eluding our grasp. We get ahold of a bit of it, either a slight grasp of its pointed and interesting texture or a little taste of its spiciness. We're touched for a moment, then as soon as we look for more, it's not to be found—flattened to the point where it's unrecognizable, or squandered on who knows what, or left untended to the point where its flame dies or its saltiness dissipates from exposure to the elements. And it's been this way from the start, with few signs of lasting correction.

A few years ago the Lilly Endowment funded a long-term study intended to come to some conclusions about the three-decades-old decline in church participation and Christian commitment among the historic, sometimes called "mainline," Protestant groups in America: the Presbyterians, the Methodists, the Lutherans, the Episcopalians, the Congregationalists. You may know the bunch. The scholars working on this project took the Presbyterian experience as a telling example, from which they were to generalize their findings. This research resulted in a series titled The Presbyterian Presence.[1]

After exhaustive study of the Presbyterian experience, replete with statistics and interviews with persons once inside and now outside the denomination, the researchers came to a simple conclusion. Their conclusions countered the assumptions of many that the purity of "mainline" purposes and the challenging rightness of "mainline" theology had sent folks running for easier religion. They also contradicted the pervasive view that folks want less, not more, and the view that congregations who emphasize feelings over content have been stealing "mainline" folk away. The research discovered that the vast majority of those who have drifted away have done so not because they've been offended or have been stolen. They did not leave for greener religious pastures. They just left. And they went nowhere. They wandered away because they were bored. On the whole, you see, the burning questions people had brought with them to church were systematically left unanswered by the very churches into which they brought their questions.

What were those questions the churches left unanswered? Put most simply, they were these: Is it true? Is the story of a God suffering out of love for humanity, saving folk from themselves, dealing with the evil of the world right at its heart, calling us into communion, giving us power to live reordered lives together, and offering favor beyond our comprehension: Is this story true? And if it is true, what am I to do about it? Like Paul's questions when he was blinded by the presence of Jesus on his way to Damascus (Who are you? And what am I to do?), too few churches acknowledged the questions, and therefore too much preaching, teaching, and mission missed the point. We simply depended too much on people bringing the real thing in with them and forgot that more often than not, folks come with an ember that needs stoking rather than a bonfire already ablaze.

Presbyterian pastor and former president of Eastern College Roberta Hestenes speaks of her upbringing in an atheistic home.[2] She was forbidden to go to church and discouraged from even entertaining the possibility of the truth of the Christian story. When in college, she experienced a lasting conversion to Christian faith. She tells of the words her father said regarding her new faith. "How could this have happened? I thought we taught you better! You know, maybe I should have sent you to church after all. This probably would never have happened if we'd sent you to church as a child!"

Odd, isn't it, that this aggressively anti-Christian parent somehow suspected that even better than his prohibition, the finest inoculation against the real thing of Christianity is often the church itself? "If I'd only sent you to church, this never would have happened." There are wonderful and plentiful exceptions to that assumption, for sure, but too often the story is true. We've got the pure stuff, and we've lived it, but too often we allow it to slip through our fingers, and we slowly learn to be content with what's far from real. And we offer others even less. The fire seems too hot, the light too bright, the possibilities too wild, the demands too great.

Now the Presbyterians may have their peculiar version of this problem, but they're not alone. For there isn't a tradition in the church that doesn't have its own way of settling with less. Still, we shouldn't kick ourselves too much for this. We've something to do with it, to be sure, but God doesn't really help too much. I mean, it seems that almost every time we get a glimpse of this pure stuff and so sense God, and not just the idea of God, in our midst, the very Spirit we glimpse seems to withdraw. It is as though God plays with us, letting us in far enough so we know what we don't have but not far enough to get a hold on it. And so it is easy to be left with what James Loder called convictional neurosis.[3] You sense it, even think you know it, but then lose its hold. Then you can't decide whether to live as though it exists or not. Who would blame you for trying to get out of the game of cat and mouse and simply order your spiritual life in ways that only *mimic* the real thing? You don't want to be too threatened by faith or too easily hurt by high expectations. It's like feeling heartbreak and not wanting to be vulnerable again; only it's deeper than that. It's God, after all.

Consider ancient Israel. The trouble appears right from the start, as early as the calling out of Egypt. Moses leads them. The sea is parted, their oppressor defeated, a promising future held out like a carrot, and they're left to wander in the wilderness for forty years. Or think of the story Israel told of the origins of our condition: Eve and Adam given the blessings of God and yet not allowed to know those blessings as blessings. In order to know, they eat of knowledge against God's wishes as though it were the sweet fruit of rebellious desire. The moment they know evil well enough to also know goodness, they are banished from the garden of innocence and left to nurture what morsels they have remaining (Genesis 2–3).

So too the church. It has written its memories of God well enough so that in reading and rereading them, as Scripture, it might be blessed enough to get another glimpse or hear another word. It forms habits, which we call liturgies, hoping to keep God in mind long enough so that when the Holy Spirit happens we worshipers might recognize the Spirit for who he is, if we're lucky.

It's understandable that we bumble about. We're trying to tame the very presence of our Creator and respond—carefully, reasonably, responsibly, enthusiastically, respectfully, humbly, rightly, joyfully, and a bit fearfully—to what we've heard, and maybe experienced. This is too big a task not to be riddled with confusion, and it holds out too glorious a possibility not to cause us to try to calm things down a bit.

You see, we're a lot like Peter. At the highest point of his Lord's ministry, when the crowds were greatest and the miracles were happening without pause, and when by all accounts their stock was soaring, the most profound insight of all came to Peter in a flash (Mark 8:27–30). Jesus is asking around, "Who do people say that I am?" And he's hearing the acceptable terms of the day: "Your ministry is like John the Baptizer's!" "You're Elijah the prophet returned to us as promised!" "You're yet another one in the long chain of prophets God has sent to us!" Then Jesus challenges those closest to him with the same question. Peter responds, "You are the Messiah, the Christ of God." He sees it and says it with sheer abandon. And then Jesus tells them all to be quiet, as though the truth would be too much if it gets out, and as though the truth requires a much slower sort of revelation and realization than what Peter's enthusiasm can bear. And then to add insult to injury, Jesus tells them what lies ahead of this realization—suffering, scandal, arrest, and execution. Hardly the stuff one might expect after such a miraculous insight.

From the highest height to the lowest depth. And less than a week later, it happens again. Jesus takes Peter, with James and John, away from the others and up a mountain. And before their eyes he is changed, "transfigured," so the story goes. His clothes become brighter than human eyes can imagine or bleach can make white. And there with Jesus come Elijah and Moses. As if to say that all of creation, the completion of the whole story of God's dealing with Israel, comes together on that spot—Moses a sign of the law, Elijah a sign of the prophets, and the Christ alongside them. All three were chatting (Matt. 17:1–8).

Though terrified, Peter actually joins in the conversation. Is he remembering Moses' experience on Mount Sinai and wondering what his own face will look like when he returns to the others? Whatever he's thinking, Peter takes the initiative and tries to hold the moment in the best way he can. Following what Israel had done in the wilderness, he offers tents to house the glory he is witnessing. One tent for Moses. One for Elijah. One for Jesus. Each prophet would be given a place on the earth in which to rest, to which the people could come and see the shining light of God revealed—or at least to which appointed messengers could come and receive new messages for the people below. Peter would harness, calm, and make the experience of God repeatable and reliable.

There's no shame in this plan. The church is often taught to laugh at Peter and think his response naive and incongruous. And yet the building of a tent to contain the movable presence of God was a perfectly appropriate idea for someone filled by stories of the Exodus from Egypt. Short of a temple, a tent will do just fine. Even in the prologue of the Gospel of John, when John describes the dwelling of the Word in the world, he says that the Word "pitched a tent among us." Peter knew his responsibilities, and it was to them that he resorted in this terrific moment. What he didn't know was what would happen next.

I've stood on one of the two hills believed to be the Mount of Transfiguration. As I climbed the hill a foggy cloud blurred my vision, as if on cue. Within a few minutes the fog cleared as quickly as it had arrived, revealing villages and olive groves below.

From light brighter than you or I can imagine to a fog so dense that no one can see. That's what Peter saw. Exaggerated, perhaps, but nonetheless fitting for the way in which our own spirits move back and forth sometimes—bright light and fog. And in the fog, a word is sometimes heard: "This one you saw in the brightness, this my child, my beloved Son, listen to him."

As the fog disappears as quickly as it comes, only Jesus remains—no glow, no tent. And down the mountain we go. Seems that Jesus, the Christ, is also Moses and Elijah together. Brighter and warmer and clearer and holier and more visible than what Peter, James, and John could ever imagine. And this is the same Jesus Mary nursed as a baby; the same Jesus on whose feet the woman broke the bottle of oil; the same Jesus Martha served and from whom another Mary sat and learned; and the same Jesus Peter rebuked for saying he would suffer. This is the same Jesus one of the Marys saw outside the tomb on Easter morning, and the same resurrected Jesus who came among the fearful and huddling disciples in a walk-up room and gave them the power they needed to make the church. This is the Jesus with whom Peter and the others came down from the mountain and with whom they walked toward all that lay ahead in Jerusalem. This back and forth between the light and the fog can make things unpredictable and sometimes frustrating, but it's the very back and forth by which God seems to be revealed in Scripture.

We're too fragile to touch electricity, for we know that too great a jolt might throw us across the room. And yet we light darkened homes and sanctuaries and streets with it. We're too fleshy to jump into fire, and yet without fire we would die. There's the triangle. For Christian faith is not one-dimensional. It isn't enough to ask, "How might I know God?" and not ask, "How then am I to live day to day?" Nor is it enough to ask, "What am I to do day today?" without also asking, "Who is this God?" We are turned from the brightness and pushed down the mountain toward the world in which we live. And if we watch closely enough, the world in which we live will raise for us enough questions and desires for something more that we can't help but look again toward the shielded brightness on the mountain, through the fog. This is what I am saying, in one way or another, in nearly every chapter of this book.

The church has always believed that we can't really love each other unless our love is a redirection of our love for God. And the church has also always believed that there is no love of God that is not manifest, somehow, through and in the ordinary relationships of life. It's not one or the other: reasonable order or spiritual chaos, God's time or our time, God's money or our money, mission or program, belief or unbelief. It is all transformed, "transfigured," so the Scriptures say, into God's way hidden in the world.

Morton Kelsey discusses research about a reality in our churches that I believe is clear to anyone looking.[4] That reality is that the majority of folks, even among those who remain in the declining "mainline," have at some point or another had what they believed to be a significant experience of God: care during a time of crisis that you just knew, without explanation, was from a source beyond; the voice of another person that you just knew was speaking a deeper word; a room filled with light in the middle of the night, when all the lights were turned off; a healing after prayer that stumped the doctors; a relationship reconciled that you had thought was gone or a sin forgiven that you thought was indelible; the power to bear the weight of circumstances beyond your control without falling apart. Or peace at death. Or warmth moving through your body from the tip of your head to your toes. Or a firm knowledge that the road you've turned on toward Christian living is the beginning of full life. Or freedom from a habit that would destroy you. Or the courage to face the injustice and the pain and the hurt in the world. Or the gift of joy in the midst of it all. Or the blessed discovery that others are there too. You have experienced these things, or have heard reliable testimony from others.

Yet there is another reality on which Kelsey reports that many also know well. And that is that there are not enough good and safe ways in the church to talk about these transfiguring experiences. There are surely dimensions of our experiences of God that are so close that they would best remain between us and God or shared only with a trusted pastor or counselor. Yet there are also dimensions of these experiences that must be shared more openly if they are to become the gift to the church that they actually are. Perhaps Peter was not allowed to build his tents because *we* must build them in the worlds in which we live. And we must build them in a way that neither stifles God by insisting that God can only happen in extravagant experiences, nor forgets God by insisting that only ordinary life is trustworthy.

Fact is, you see, we've not been set up at all. We've actually been set free to live, in whatever circumstances we find ourselves, in this triangle of spirituality: the transfiguring experience of God, the tough day to day, and the witness of faith. And there's freedom indeed, not in resolving the problem but in living with others in the middle. So I believe.

10

Against Heroes

Mark 10:35–45

In the introduction to this book I used a parable from Søren Kierkegaard. Let me adapt another one here. It seems that in the magnificent cathedral, the Honorable and Right Reverend Geheime-General-Ober-Hof-Pradikant, the elect favorite of the fashionable world, appears before an elect company and preaches with emotion on the text he himself elected: "God hath elected the base things of the world, and the things that are despised." And nobody laughs.[1]

Now let me try another story, from the Gospel of Mark. Seems Zebedee's boys, James and John, sense some tension as Jesus turns away from his long ministry in Galilee and the outer towns to head toward Jerusalem. We're on the edge of the most important turning in the adventures of Jesus. The rhythms of preaching and teaching, confusions and insights, healings and exorcisms, conspiracies and intimacies that filled his short years of ministry now shift to a surer and steadier movement. The invocation of Jerusalem always seems to heighten tension. It'll be a long march up. And the Passover scene awaits, which opens to political intrigue, religious crisis, execution, and, to everyone's surprise but God's, a resurrection. (I imagined the circus of that time in chapter 6.)

A swift drama of cosmic significance will mark our way in. We know this now, as readers and hearers of the story. But in the account as we have it in Mark, James and John didn't know it yet. They only know something is up. The moment sits on the watershed of Mark's gospel and gives readers the chance to make the same choice it forces on James and John.

Let me set the stage. These brothers had been with Jesus from the start. And they remained with Jesus, despite their anxieties, all the way down. They were two of the three with whom Jesus chose to go up the hill when Elijah and Moses appeared (Matt. 17:1–8). They became pivotal leaders in the early church. And we count them among our parents in the faith. Apparently, they were the kind of siblings who liked to be together and watch out for each other. Get one, get both. They had a partnership. And they were also the kind who tend to be a step or two ahead of others. Futurists. Intuitionists. Co-chairs of the long-range planning committee.

"Keep your ears to the ground."

"Keep abreast of the latest developments."

"Subscribe to those market climate newsletters that promise to help you make a profit in a bear market."

I infer all of this because talking between themselves about all that was happening, these two hatched a little plan. "We're heading into Jerusalem, and things are going to change. Isn't it like Jesus to be coy? Must mean something. By all indications it seems like big possibilities. If the crowds appear as the rumors say they will, and if they pull Jesus into the revolution as the rumors say some of them want to do, then this intimate little family thing we've got going isn't going to last. So if we're going to keep it going without him, it'll need to be ordered properly. Someone will have to speak for Jesus and make decisions when he is busy with other matters. If we don't make transition plans now, we'll be caught by surprise later." A bit like getting in on the ground floor of a marginal political campaign only to discover that your candidate might actually win. You suddenly have to adapt to notoriety.

So clipboards in hand: "Jesus, do you have a minute? Now, don't say no right away . . . promise you'll say yes or at least consider what we have in mind."

And Jesus smiles, not unlike a kind and challenging mother in the presence of a precocious child. "Yes, sweet child? What do you need?"

"Well, now, Lord, hear us out. When it all happens, we mean, when you come into your glory—which we believe you will—you'll need to reorganize all of this. We want to help. For this is a precious and powerful thing we have among the twelve of us, with you, and research shows that charismatic leaders tend to need help with institutionalizing their visions. Here's our idea. We are willing to take leadership roles. Make us your right- and left-hand men. We were there with you on top of that mountain, and we'll be there with you no matter what. You needn't worry about a thing with us at the helm."

There are other ways to bring the passage to life, for sure, but go with this one for a moment. Jesus continues to look in that gentle, mothering way. He nods with a slight and knowing smile, taking them at face value, but of course knowing more of what they ask than they. He weighs their intentions and examines the sincerity of their hearts. He stares down into the strength of their spirits and considers the implications. And he tests their resolve.

"Well . . . okay . . . how serious are you? You will drink the same cup of wrath as me. Do you know that? And you'll be baptized by the same fire? Are you able?"

Now, don't rush to a conclusion too quickly here. For why do we tend to think these brothers fools for thinking they're ready? Perhaps they *are* ready. The story of the church is full of believing folk and faithful groups, most of whose names we don't remember and whose stories never made news beyond those who knew them. There are folks who have said yes in true, careful, and resolved ways, even in our day. They may suffer for the yeses they give, but they never turn back. They hold the world, even when the world ignores them, uses them, and reviles them. Even when the church fails them. You may be among them.

James and John surely did not understand the full meaning of what they sought, but they may well have known enough to seek it, at least if we can surmise for a moment that it wasn't mere glory they sought. And so having turned their question once, Jesus turns it again. The first turn was toward a deeper sense of what following him might mean, in time. The second turn is toward a broader sense of what following him might mean in eternity.

"Okay . . ." he says, "I believe you. Whether you believe yourselves or not, I believe you. And so you will share with me. But the final meaning of your following, in the world in which we live and in the circumstances in which we find ourselves? That you will never predict nor will you control. But that does not matter anymore, now that you've said this yes. It is your yes that matters. Leave control to God."

Why do I read this story this way, when it is most often told as a story of the disciples' naive, even arrogant, desire for their own glory? In part because of what happens next. The other ten disciples are angry with James and John, which leaves us with a puzzle. Are they angry because they're jealous and wish they'd asked first? Are they angry because James and John have asked Jesus to choose favorites among them? Are they angry because these two have raised the stakes of willingness?

Jesus responds to their anger by discussing leadership and authority, not honor and glory. And that's important, at least in the reading I am staging here. It suggests what aroused the others' anger in the first place: questions of leadership and authority. And so it suggests, by extension, that it was leadership and authority that James and John were seeking, not just eternal glory. And there's the ground for thinking that James and John were asking for something quite practical, even political.

There's Jesus, turning it all again and saying to all twelve of
them, "We do not live by an ethic foreign to God's people. Because of this, a summons to lead need not be feared. Nor should
even an offer to lead. James and John ask only to serve. They're
not politicians, after all. So give them no mind." In other words,
"Forget your squabbling over who's in charge. Remember who
you are and get on to the business of what to do. For when you
drink my communion cup or take my baptismal bath, you learn
quickly, if you learn at all, that position and prestige and practical
power come and go. And they are fickle for reasons we cannot
finally control, nor should want to control. You may be there
or you may not, and frankly that is irrelevant to your ability to
serve as I ask you to. And no matter who's on top or who's next
in line, you may still find ways to follow me. And you may yet
find your way to places you never imagined you'd go. You may
find your way to experiences you never imagined you'd have,
or to a love for the world, in all its pain and all its wonder, that
you never understood before. You may find a simple peace that
frees you to give peace to others in a way you never thought you
could. Don't worry yourselves with James and John, for they have
already chosen the better part by saying yes to me. And you may
do the same. For whoever wishes to become great among you
must be your servant, and whoever wishes to be first among you
must be slave of all. For the Son of Man came not to be served
but to serve, and to give his life a ransom for many" (paraphrase
of Mark 10:43–45).

Count this as joy, not worry. For if the sort of leadership I describe is one of individual heroes drinking Christ's cup and taking
the heat alone, I have not made my point very well. Following
Jesus need not, necessarily, mean walking between the lines of
fire to imitate his public sacrifice. One should never exclude that
possibility, but that's not the call, first off. The call, first off, is
this: to join with others and follow the suffering of Jesus on its
own terms, and to let the ransom that Jesus paid do its work to

free us from the things that hold hostage our freedom to live and act in the ways of holy love. Let Jesus lead, and let his Spirit put you where you need to be: before a child, alongside a colleague, part of a machine that makes a difference, or in a place to make positive change in some system of commerce or education or government or church. Or in struggles for integrity and patience in the burdens of day-to-day living. Or with your own self, on the better side of the battles that rage in your body or your spirit. Or with folks who are close. Christ addresses us, face to face, in those places. And it is in those places that we might begin again to see, and we might begin again to follow, in order to begin again to serve. Serve in the places closest to you, often hidden from public view. Let other kinds of service come and go as they will. Seek leadership it if it is given you. Don't worry if it is given to someone else. And if it is given to someone else, pray for them, and ask them to pray for you.

And no one laughs at Kierkegaard's elect Right Reverend, indeed. This may be because we're blind to our own foolishness and look far too much like him ourselves. Yet it may also be because when living in the face of Christ, we finally see through our foolishness to something greater.

"What is it you want me to do for you?" Jesus asks.

11

On Martin Luther King Jr.: Self-Dispense or Self-Defense

Matthew 5:38–48 and 1 Peter 3:9

Do not repay evil for evil or abuse for abuse; but, on the contrary, repay with a blessing.

1 PETER 3:9 NRSV

In each of my years as a college chaplain, I was one of a group responsible for planning campus events to celebrate the birthday of Martin Luther King Jr. As long as I was there, I used whatever influence I had to insist that one of the principal centers of the celebration be the college chapel, for King was a minister of the gospel, and his movement was primarily a movement for reform within the church. It took place on a secular stage, but it was addressed to the conscience of Christians.

We welcomed Andrew Young into a packed chapel one year. On another year, we hosted Gideon Makanya, who had been a leader in the Standing for the Truth Campaign in South Africa as the secretary of the Black Baptist Church of South Africa. We founded the College-Community Gospel Ensemble during one of those celebrations. The college brought guest choirs from King's alma mater, Morehouse College, and the sister school to Morehouse, Spellman College, at other times. We also found ways to bring ministers and lay people from two predominantly black churches in the area into closer association with the college community. We had public readings of King's sermons and speeches, and candlelight services. These were good times.

Finally one year, after the faculty of the college elected to take up its long-neglected right to become more involved in the planning for this holiday, strenuous objections were raised to our chapel activities. "No one should be forced to enter a Christian sanctuary to celebrate the heritage of King," these voices claimed. "Do your chapel service if you want, but we won't list it as an official event of the college." So it went, and the official gaze of the college turned elsewhere.

We worshiped anyway and had a good time. But in turning their attention away, I believe that the leaders of the college lost hold of something true and abiding about King. For despite all attempts to think otherwise, King's work was inconceivable outside the church.

Now there is no question that the King holiday was declared for largely political, rather than religious, reasons—justifiable political reasons, perhaps, but political nevertheless. And the church of Christ can pick and choose in which political arguments it wants to participate. But we would be foolish to ignore the opportunity—no, the gift—the church has been given in the King holiday. For on that day, the nation celebrates a faithful and prophetic child of the church. On that holiday, the nation celebrates a life that takes many of the contradictions of our culture and lays them before the cross.

Others whom we celebrate with holidays—Columbus, Washington, Lincoln—attempted to interpret their work through the Christian gospel. But King—here was a preacher. Here was a person whose public words and actions were consumed with releasing the power of gospel truth and gospel love. In 1963, King put it quite simply: "I have sought to bring the Christian message to bear on the social evils that cloud our days and the personal witness and disciplines required."[1] What better summary? He was not infallible, but he was inspired of God.

I believe it's time the whole church took King in, reclaiming the Christian substance of his message. We want to say that his message, beyond simply a strategy to produce political ends, was prophecy. And we want to say that his work, beyond simply leading a social movement, was gospel ministry.

We need to remember King's ministry and find ways to teach it to our youth as a vital episode of church history. And we need to find in that memory some truths of the gospel we may too easily forget. I believe that Martin Luther King Jr. may stand with Billy Graham as one of the two most significant religious figures in twentieth-century America, however one feels about their messages.

One of those truths of King that we too easily forget is how thoroughgoing and expansive is the New Testament call to renounce violence as a way of being and doing in the world. King reminded his hearers of Jesus' command to turn the other cheek. He also reminded them of Peter's insistence that one of the preconditions for church, one of the marks of citizenship in God's realm, is the disciplined refusal to exchange evil for evil.

Yes, King's nonviolence was an effective method of suing for social reform. He first learned of its political potency, and of the philosophy that undergirded its strength, from Gandhi. He chiseled it into its American expression in Montgomery, Alabama, and polished it throughout the land. But we would be remiss if we left our investigation there, quarantining the challenge of nonviolence within those moments of history and in those towns. We would be remiss to assume that the call to nonviolence, while certainly good and easy to affirm for folks who are oppressed and need justice, isn't particularly relevant to everyone. What a mistake that would be. For when King adapted Gandhi's method in Montgomery, he tapped into a deep well of New Testament truth everyone is free to drink from, and he rediscovered an image of Christian togetherness that remains a central New Testament image of a faithful church.

The Hindu Gandhi taught King about the force of love—what appears to be an almost violent force—that is released when one joins with others and refuses to return evil for evil. Gandhi himself called the New Testament the book that had influenced him more than any other. The love force he taught King recalled the church, not without pain, to the witness and discipline that marks New Testament faithfulness.

Already in his late twenties, King was learning that nonviolence is finally more than a method. It is a conversion. Read his words:

> The experience in Montgomery did more to clarify my thinking in regard to the question of nonviolence than all of the books that I had read. As the days unfolded, I became more and more convinced of the power of nonviolence. Nonviolence became more than a method to which I gave intellectual assent; it became a commitment to a way of life. Many issues I had not cleared up intellectually concerning nonviolence were now resolved within the sphere of practical action. . . . The nonviolent approach does something to the hearts and souls of those committed to it. It gives them self-respect. It calls up resources of strength and courage that they did not know that they had. Finally, it so stirs the conscience of the opponent that reconciliation becomes a reality.[2]

Reconciliation is possible because Jesus sits right there in the conscience of the church, just as he sits right there in the individual consciences of Christian people. He sits right there and calls us away from the cycle of revenge and retribution that has so indelibly marked human experience. Jesus sits right there, as if saying, "Remember me; remember that I have ended all of this and freed you from the need for revenge. Find your power to forgive, repent, reconcile, here, in my bosom. Find that love force here, and speak truth to the world wisely and unafraid."

The New Testament call to nonviolence is unequivocal and unmistakable. It's like a wager right at the heart of Scripture, betting everything that the power of forgiveness, repentance, and reconciliation can create a church more faithful to Christ than can ideas or methods alone. You see, this New Testament nonviolence is more than a principle or an idea or even a working theology. It's a practice. As we continually admit failure, it bears us up and pushes us forward toward new ways of being with each other. Whether we're liberal or conservative, black or white, young or old, woman or man, this wager on the power of forgiveness and repentance has the potential to significantly change our lives.

I am convinced, and I write and preach and teach to give testimony to the prospect that Jesus means what he says when he says:

> You have heard that it was said to those of ancient times, "You shall not murder"; and "whoever murders shall be liable to judgment." But I say to you that if you are angry with a brother or sister, you will be liable to judgment; and if you insult a brother or sister, you will be liable to the council; and if you say, "You fool," you will be liable to the hell of fire.
>
> MATTHEW 5:21–22 NRSV

> You have heard that it was said, "You shall love your neighbor and hate your enemy." But I say to you, Love your enemies and pray for those who persecute you, so that you may be children of your Father in heaven.
>
> MATTHEW 5:43–45 NRSV

I am also convinced that the author of 1 Peter was inspired when writing, "Do not repay evil for evil or abuse for abuse; but, on the contrary, repay with a blessing. It is for this that you were called" (3:9 NRSV).

The easiest response would be to soften this call, to qualify it by noting reasonable exceptions. "Sure, it's good to temper our tempers and seek peace when we can. But there are times, you know, when one must defend oneself, or one's family, or one's nation, or one's race, or one's gender, or one's livelihood, or one's whatever when violence gets too close and too threatening. We don't like it, but sometimes you just can't avoid it. You can't tell me never to be angry, after all. You can't tell me that revenge is never called for or that a proportional response to evil is not sometimes prudent!"

"How destructive to victims," you say to me, "to withhold from them the freedom to lash out when necessary. This unqualified prohibition on reasonable violence can be bad for the pitiable and overwhelmed folk of the world: women, children, poor families, oppressed peoples, folks sometimes hurt by powers they can't control. "Moreover," you go on, "the freedom to use violence is a necessary tool in the arsenal of those more powerful to whom the task of keeping order has been given."

No doubt. I too can think of situations in which it seems right to wish for a benign power to intervene, even by force, to stop evildoing. But there Jesus sits, God among us accepting our violence and working to transform it, even violence that seems taken as a last resort. The call to the church is, first, to cry out against violence. It should very reluctantly allow violence as a tool, if it allows it at all. For the church is surely aware of the human tendency to take on the character of our tools. Hold the sword and you risk becoming the sword. Before taking its rightful place at the table of political theory and policy making, therefore, the onus is on the church to gather round Christ and to prayerfully create both a real space and an imagined realm where violence is less and less necessary and the unequivocal New Testament call can be lived out more and more joyfully. This is the task that

Stanley Hauerwas calls creating a new politics, not in order to be political but to humble the political for the sake of hope.[3]

Christians believe (or so I hope) that despite our experience to the contrary, the cycle of violence and retribution came to a head when we tried to kill God. Christians believe that despite appearances to the contrary, the crucifixion of Jesus was, and will remain, the most violent act of human experience. Christians believe that there we attacked and attempted to overthrow the very love that created us, and yet God accepted such violence and finally overturned it.

Now in the wake of Christ's death and resurrection, believers no longer need feel bound to violence. They are bound to a new, though ancient, love, and they are propelled by that love into a new way of being with others. The church is meant to show that new way of being to the world—by applying to ourselves the same standards we apply to others, and by confronting evil without participating in it, however weak or strong we may be. No more boundaries of violence are necessary for protection, whether those boundaries are constructed by physical might, ritualized revenge, or verbal retribution. These are necessary no longer. What a treat. Sarcasm, gone. Backbiting, gone. Gossip, gone. Game playing and manipulation, gone. Defensiveness, why? Weapons, banished. Lying or oversimplifying the past, irrelevant. Gathering allies rather than friends, ridiculous. Refusing to confess, to seek forgiveness and to forgive, sad. Missing the challenge and wonderful joy of this new way of living, tragic.

There are so many stories one can tell, examples of the ordinary and extraordinary moments of life in which people have harnessed the power of God to end the cycle of revenge and live into the new reality Christ offers. But I want to tell one story, long forgotten until it came to mind during one of those college chapel gatherings for King. I remembered a newspaper clipping that had yellowed in a bureau drawer. I believe it was taken from the *Daily Tribune* in Royal Oak, Michigan. I grew up in Royal Oak and remember when a little girl was murdered in some woods. I would dare predict that everyone who lived in that town at that time also remembers her body found in those woods, the fear that went through the heart of every parent, the sorrow and anger, the hatred for her violator, and the nearly universal desire for revenge. As I recall it, a young man was arrested for the murder. The parents of the girl agreed to an interview, words from which I paraphrase from the fragility of memory. "We are Christian people," they allowed. "We do not want revenge. We pray for the man who murdered our daughter, for we have no other choice. We pray that God might forgive him, and that he might grant us the strength to one day forgive him ourselves. And we pray that he might know Jesus and find salvation in him, and find true peace. And we pray that one day, by God's mercy, we will sit together at table with our daughter, and with him, in heaven."

There was a witness in that story deep enough to prompt a ten-year-old boy to take scissors and cut that article from the paper. For there it was, a sign that there might be something about the faith, and about this thing called church, worth paying attention: to the "witness and discipline required," as it is described in 1 Peter 3:9.

As King's followers gathered in church basements, and sang hymns and spirituals together, and read Scripture together, and prayed together, and stood up together, and accepted the water cannons and gunfire together, they knew the power of Jesus to make them a church. And they knew that no one could do anything worse to them than what all of us had done to God when we hung Jesus on a tree. And because of that, they knew that the power of God in the resurrection of Jesus was available as much today as it was then. And they knew, when grace allowed, that when they were able to embrace white Christians and call them sisters and brothers, God was alive and was powerful enough to make a church again. Just peace can finally be imagined when such a church is born.

By the power of God, it is possible to confront evil without participating in it or being forever changed by it. And by the power of God, it is possible to learn how to live nonviolently in the ordinariness of living, applying to oneself the same standards one applies to others.

And by the power of God, it is possible to fully embody and enjoy the habits of Christian living that continually call us back to the wager that Jesus won—confession, repentance, and reconciliation, even if only, for now, reconciliation with God.

In 1960, Martin Luther King Jr. said, "There are some who still find the cross a stumbling block, and others consider it foolishness, but I am more convinced than ever before that it is the power of God unto social and individual salvation. So like the Apostle Paul I can now humbly yet proudly say, 'I bear in my body the marks of the Lord Jesus.' . . . More than ever before I am convinced of the reality of a personal God."[4]

May we come to know what King knew.

12

Gifts That Work

Romans 12

A little thing happened one Valentine's Day in the Avram household that taught me a religious lesson. My wife and I had been mulling over what to do for a dinner that evening for the two of us after her attempts to secure a babysitter had failed. I had been out running some errands and returned home ready to continue the conversation about what I should go out and get for the evening, so I could quickly get back to working on a sermon or something. I walked in the back door of the house to discover my wife and an old friend of hers standing in the kitchen chatting. We had returned to the area just a few months before and to our delight found that this friend lived just a few blocks away. She stood with a cardboard box in front of her. We all chatted a while longer, mostly small talk, when she picked up the box and handed it to Lynne. "I was out picking up some dinner when I saw this and thought of you. Happy Valentine's Day!" Pause. "Be careful!"

We gingerly slipped the box open to discover a wiggling lobster. As you can imagine, we had a good laugh. We had just moved from Maine, you see, where even license plates had lobsters on them. A kettle of boiling water, a little homemade slaw, some drawn butter with lemon juice, a lit candle and a bottle of wine, and Valentine's dinner was served.

No reason for the gift. It was a surprise that at first seemed an interruption but proved to be a gift that made the day. And I considered my first, all-too-human response. I had searched my mind to figure out if we should have bought *her* something and felt a little embarrassment that we hadn't. Now mind you, this giver was a friend but not someone with whom we'd been in the habit of exchanging valentines. The gift was given without expectation of return. It was only I who wanted to draw it back toward the rules of interpersonal commerce. How long does it take to learn not only how to give, but also how to receive?

Later that evening, I flipped on my email and discovered a message from a former colleague in Maine.[1] She was writing to a long list of friends around the country to ask our help. "As you all know," she said, "my son is now in Tennessee for a while. He's having his tenth birthday at the end of the month. Would you mind taking the time to send him a postcard from where you live? I want him to get a big pile of cards with pictures from all over the country so he knows how many people know about him and care about him." My first thought? "This an awfully nice idea, but do I have time for this?" Then I recalled the event of the afternoon, and I realized that I *should* have time for this. Responding to one gift with another, directed elsewhere, to a place the first giver knows nothing of. It's the chain of gift giving, both mundane and significant, that makes life full. Our friend with the lobster might not know that the best gift she gave, at least to me, quite unintentionally, was a reminder that I too have the time to give in ways that seek no return. Don't get me wrong, the lobster was tasty, but her reminder was the greatest gift.

As in many households in which a home was made on one income, money was tight when I was a child. My parents had a habit that is repeated in other families, I'm sure. They added a feel of abundance to gift giving and managed to divert tight resources toward the children by folding necessities into their rituals of gift giving. If either of them discovered in October that they had an irreparable hole in their winter gloves, for example, or that they needed new socks or hose, they would get by for a few weeks until their necessities became a gift under the Christmas tree. This was especially true for the parents, but sometimes true for the children as well. It wasn't unusual to see a snow shovel waiting there under the tree, all shiny and with a red bow. Not quite the romantic gift of Bloomingdale's commercials. Yet alongside all these things that needed to be purchased anyway, now dressed up to appear special, was always one or two more surprising items. As I grew older I began to understand this practice as part of living on a budget, but when I was younger I absorbed a different, and perhaps more valuable, lesson. For as a child, this practice was not about household income at all. It was about the nature of gifts, and I think it taught something profoundly Christian without our knowing it: if we've a grateful heart, even the most mundane and seemingly ordinary thing can be treated like the gift it truly is.

I hear tell of an old man, now long dead, who raised hybrid roses as a hobby in southern Michigan. I'm told that one of his favorite sayings was, "If I had fifty cents to my name, with a quarter I'd buy a loaf of bread, and with a quarter I'd buy a rose." Now that's the way you respond to a gift, whether it's a gift you discover in yourself or a gift handed you from another: a loaf of bread in one hand and a rose in the other. The mark of a gifted life.

But how are we to think about giving and receiving in a culture hell-bent on convincing us that all gift giving is to be brought into the marketplace of purchased happiness? In a world in which you and I are taught that everything is a need and few things are gifts, when everything from Cuisinarts to cell phones, from therapists to personal trainers, and from SAT preparation courses to annual vacations are considered coins of contentment, it's genuinely hard to give and receive gifts in the way the church has tried to affirm. We do it, thank God, but it's hard.

The man who bought the rose was not purchasing his happiness. He purchased the rose because he already had his happiness, as a gift from elsewhere. This is what the church calls blessedness—or giftedness.

When Olympic athletes are commercially sponsored and professionally trained before they're even teenagers, it's hard to remember that the simple use of an arm or a leg is a gift from beyond us.

And when nearly every street corner has a coffee shop, or a fast-food joint, or a bakery, or a grocery store with shelves overflowing, it's hard to fully appreciate the gift of a piece of bread and a glass of wine or cup of tea.

And when one of the visions ruling our day is of every twelve-year-old plugged into the Internet and every eighteen-year-old enrolled in some form of tuition-driven schooling, it's hard to experience our simple, unschooled abilities as gifts in and of themselves—like our ability to observe and tell stories or imagine possible worlds. And it's hard to accept the possibility still believed by the church, that the collection of books called the Bible is in fact a more marvelous gift to the future than the World Wide Web. Christian blessedness begins with the recognition that the simplest gifts of life are from God. It then extends outward to re-create experience in its image.

What will life be like when our God-given freedom to live as gifted and gifting people is finally taken from us by the market? I choose to believe that won't happen, because I can't imagine life that way.

A longtime member of my congregation died the same week we received that lobster. I had met her only a couple of times, but I thought about what little I did know about her. I thought about stories our pastor for congregational care told of his visits with her and what others told of their encounters with her. I observed her extended family of three sons with families of their own. This story can be repeated in many families, but the connection of her dying and the idea of gift giving deserves comment. For even before meeting the family, I had already heard stories of her joyful readiness to die, about the way in which she had grasped the important Christian work of dying well. She was ready to "be with God," she'd tell her visitors, even while she was happy to make plans for an even longer life here if that was in store. That readiness to die gave her courage to live life with grace and acceptance toward others. One of her sons put it like this: "She had passed through a period of troubled questioning, and even a little fear of the beyond, to a comforted confidence in what lay ahead for her, and on to a happy looking-forward. She brought others with her. Don't think we're not sad, but her dying is also a gift." And her wake became a celebration, characteristically Christian, full of art and grace and giftedness. Most of us are losing that art of living that can make even dying a gift. She had not.

I suppose that I should return to reality here, for I know well enough that gifts remain tokens of exchange in late capitalist society. We think of gifts as relationship money and calculate their appropriateness in those terms. We want to know what's expected of us by someone who gives us something. We worry over missing the cues that tell us when gift-giving is appropriate and when it is not, and how the transaction is to be performed. The sharing of our skills, our resources, our time, and even our commitments is carefully negotiated through unspoken rules. These rules can make for peaceful, predictable, and relatively fulfilling relationships. I wouldn't disparage them, except to note how fragile they are. As much as they make for predictability, they can also be misinterpreted and misused, especially in a multicultural society. It takes patience to negotiate this kind of gift giving. Yet as all the stories told here recall, there may yet be something in us that wants to think of gifts as things passed between people that are unearned, neither negotiated nor exchanged for value.

I want to think of gifts as symbols of good feeling, regard, and respect that require no return, as symbols whose power as gifts is drawn from a place beyond the relationship between the giver and the receiver. I want to imagine gift giving as an action that has a purpose in itself, not as some means to an end. I want it to be special, personal, and a surprise. And I want that gift giving to call us beyond ourselves and in fact to re-create us in the giving and receiving.

Do we not live with a Christian memory of a kind of worship and a kind of living together that are something more than the arrangement of power for material ends? Have we not been given a memory of sheer abundance, of what Christian tradition calls God's good gift of creation? Is there not something moving about a scene of gift giving in which there is such joy in both the giving and the receiving that an onlooker can't tell who is the giver and who the receiver? Gifting, if you'll allow the verb, is both a loaf of bread and a rose. Such interweaving is at the heart of Christian community and is the gifting that makes church. Each kind of gift giving changes the other when it is exercised in the Spirit.

Christians see gifts everywhere. The language becomes familiar. The most ordinary things, like pieces of bread and small cups of wine, or like our ability to be present to each other, or our freedom to make a public declaration of our intention to call ourselves Christian—the church calls these things gifts. They are both ordered and regular parts of this culture called the church and extravagant, undeserved, special, and very personal creations of God. They are pressed right down and set in our laps.

If their gatherings are indeed exercised in the Spirit, Christian congregations will come to believe that their fellowship has a certain miraculous quality about it. The miraculous quality is precisely that wonderful mixture of ordinary freedom and extraordinary giftedness. And this miracle is completed when the gifts we are to each other, despite our humanness, are transformed by Christ into a gift to the world.

The apostle Paul sees this kind of gifting at the heart of Christian community, and folks are still trying to grasp his description of it. Paul sees *gifting*—a pure and gracious, undeserved and holy, God-derived and powerfully creative surprise at the center of what makes church. While this gifting is indeed supernatural for Paul, it is not free-floating or detached from history. It can be located in time and lives in memory. It is touchable in the repeated actions of those who live as church in relation to it. It is the life, death, and resurrection of Christ, Lord of the church. And it is present to the church, in time, as the Holy Spirit.

This is so real for Paul that it has profoundly practical implications. It makes for a community life that is patterned to imitate and protect the grace that creates it. And it becomes a gift to the world by being transparent to God's gift to the world in Jesus. We are transparent to God's gift in Jesus by giving and receiving gifts in such a way that the world remembers Jesus when it watches us, and by our living lives so deeply changed by grace that the world notices and may begin to wonder about the story of resurrection we tell. And we do this by loving in ways so directed that what the world calls need becomes God's strange gift for human solidarity and compassion, thus, again, revealing God's solidarity and compassion for the world in Christ. We do this by finding ways of showing each other who we really are so deeply and patiently that God's desire for the good of all creation can be spied. It takes hard, deliberate work to love so freely and seemingly effortlessly, but so goes the relationship between measure and abundance in the church.

Paul even uses a new word for this gifting, *charisma*. This manifests itself in spiritual gifts called *charismata*. Throughout the New

Testament, it is only in Paul that this word appears in this form. It's a mixture of *charis*, which is the grace I just described and *pneuma*, which refers to spirit. There were both wild and windy charismata, like speaking in tongues, and plain and plodding charismata, like serving meals. But note this: Paul refuses to distinguish between the seemingly ecstatic and the seemingly ordinary charismata except as they are judged by how they are used to lovingly build up the church.

When transformed by the grace and power of Christ's Spirit, all that you do can become a spiritual gift. You are free to live, in fact you are *called* to live, in such a way that even ordinary dealings are lived as gifts of love. For acts transparent to God are not necessarily otherworldly. They can be profoundly this-worldly: teaching, serving, giving money, speaking truth to a moment, encouraging others, leading with integrity, showing mercy. But they are always gifts, *charismata*, given out of the sheer abundance we call grace. They are given out of gratitude for gifts received and in ways that create a loving, truth-telling, compassionate, nonviolent, thriving church—revealing Christ.

Now this is revolutionary. It is the heart of Christian ethics.

This is gifting.

Epilogue

Preaching and Hearing
as Leaning-Toward

About an Awkward Cross

At three thousand and counting, St. Paul's Church in Rochester, Michigan, has one of the largest memberships of any United Methodist congregation in the Midwest. Its recently retired senior pastor, Dr. Timothy Hickey, was assigned to his post in the early 1970s. When he arrived, the church was maturing into its then relatively new sanctuary—a center-aisled, single-level, A-frame design rather typical of Midwestern Methodist and Presbyterian churches of that time. Just over the quarter-wall separating the altar area and the rear choir there hung a simple, good-sized cross, suspended straight in the air with its center bar aligned with the point of the angled, curtain-covered walls in the back. The small sanctuary from the 1950s had been converted into a chapel.

Come ten or twelve years into this new ministry, steady growth in membership and reliable demographics suggested it might be time to build again. St. Paul's Church took the steps growing churches of its kind normally take. Committees were formed,

planning was initiated, arguments were had, congregational meetings were scheduled, visions were shaped, drawings were commissioned, financing was strategized, and the long march toward
funding, and then building, was begun.

What came from this was a two-leveled, five-aisled, semicircular
contemporary sanctuary with a freestanding chancel. It was designed to serve eleven hundred worshipers. Through a couple of
crises along the way, such as the discovery that the construction
was sinking into an unknown water basin, and with patience,
prayer, and hard work, this new worship space was dedicated
in 1988. This is an interesting but not terribly unusual building story, except for something that happened near the end of
construction, the results of which will reverberate through that
congregation for years, or at least until they build their fourth
sanctuary.

As I understand it, at the designated moment workers were
called to bring the hanging cross over from the former sanctuary to the new one. It had been decided that both the simple
stained-glass windows and that cross over the altar would be
brought from the old space to the new space as a way of provid-
ing a sense of continuity. An affirmation of history, a way to save
a little money, and a good way to comfort those who weren't
too happy with all the changes. The cross was once again to be
hung over the altar, to the right and slightly behind the freestanding pulpit.

Watching the cross being hung, the pastor sensed something
was wrong. He called the architect for a meeting.

"Meet me in the new sanctuary when you come."

And so they met.

"Come over and stand with me here in the pews and look at
the chancel."

"Yes? What's wrong, Dr. Hickey? It looks just like we planned."

"It's not wrong. It's just not . . . right. It's the cross."

And the architect reviewed his work. "Yes? We worked hard to
arrange things as you and your committee asked. Everything is set
so the center of attention is first the hanging cross, then the altar,

then the pulpit. Choir, organ, and pipes to the left. Readers to the right. And the altar rail fits in perfectly. It's as we planned."

"I understand. I simply don't think we're saying it the way it needs to be said. I sat here yesterday. I moved around the sanctuary, back and forth, up to the balcony and down to the rail, in the choir and behind the pulpit. Then it came."

"Yes?"

"The cross doesn't wait for us. It doesn't hold back behind our tools of worship, or hide behind the way we order our lives as a church, or conform to our movement as we enter the building. It doesn't impose, but it does intrude. The cross comes to us. It's like the fire hanging over that pulpit; it should feel like it's just about to break loose and take everything in, not to destroy but to bring to life. The cross is more than a wooden sign of our memory, my friend. I want a living, surprising symbol of the Holy Spirit searching us out and pulling us to faith. My point is this: if Christ comes to us even when we think we've put him away, and if the cross in this sanctuary is a sign of this, then the cross in this sanctuary must come to us too."

"Yes?" the architect responded again.

"Yes," the pastor came back. "I want it at a definite angle, immediately noticeable but not looming or frightening. It must interrupt us and pull our attention. If it doesn't, we've failed. I want you to turn it to the left a few degrees to gesture toward the pulpit, and I want you slant it in, and then up, and just enough back so that it if you've eyes to see, it catches you up short. And I want it to feel bigger than it is, and far more ready and alive than it would be if it were just lengths of wood pieced together. And I want the angling to work so the best way to see it straight will be to kneel at the rail and look up. I'll deal with the building committee. You figure out how to do it."

"But what if it falls?"

"Who will it fall on?"

"I see. I'll have to get back to you."

And he called a couple of days later. "Can't be done. I've gone over it with our engineer and mulled it around myself, and we can't see how it can be done safely. Cross is too big, too heavy, and, frankly, I think it'll all end up just too . . . strange. Again, I'm sorry."

Tim Hickey did not accept this answer. "Well, you need to know that I'm a bit like that cross. I'm intruding on your plans and asking you to think differently. Look again, and find a way. I hope to hear from you next week with your plans."

And so the committee trusted, and the engineers finally accommodated, and if you ever visit St. Paul's Church, you'll see this cross. And it may change the way you think about such things. In a life-of-its-own way, it challenges everything. Rather like one of those icons of Jesus painted on the inside of the dome over the altar of an ancient Middle Eastern church, with the eyes of Christ looking down over the worshipers. The cross at St. Paul's is a bit subtler, but it is in that tradition.

Is this cross a different cross than the hidden cross I describe at the beginning of this book? Not really. For in the work of the Holy Spirit, the very hiddenness of the cross in the world may be the very element, or counterpart, of its intrusion. For the intrusion of the cross is both more insistent and more gentle than human intrusiveness. It is not bashful. It hunts, but it doesn't stalk. Discovering its hiddenness in the world is quite a bit like encountering it leaning in toward us. Its hiddenness is a part of its leaning.

About This Book

These biblical reflections on three realms in which to sense the promise of hope—in the Holy Spirit, in the world in which we live, and in the church of Christ—intuit something they cannot prove. They rest on an intuition that God happens—for us, in us, and among us—in the spaces of experience and thinking that are opened to us in those realms when we sense the edge of hope. They attempt to lean just a bit over that edge, inspired and held tightly by Scripture. A discerning eye may have quickly surmised that these reflections began as sermons. They did, but they now survive in that space between sermons and essays. No sermon is a sermon if not delivered to a particular people in a particular place, but there is enough of a tradition in the church of lifting such texts out of context and sharing them more broadly to justify these approximations. Yet even in that generative space in between, they may still prompt a certain challenge to how the peculiar form of Christian communication called preaching might participate in bringing us to where God happens. This epilogue takes up that challenge, within the shadow of that leaning cross.

I teach preaching. I also preach. I teach preaching not because I'm better in the classroom than I am in the pulpit, or because I belong in that place more than the other. I may in either case, or I may not. Or I may be better somewhere else altogether. That's for others to decide. I teach preaching, rather, because I have heard many, many sermons over many years, and by many preachers, and preaching still feels to me a bit like that hanging cross. I have been made by preaching. And so I have come to a contradictory conclusion: that this is both a nearly impossible art to teach, and yet for the sake of the Spirit and for the sake of the church and for the sake of the world, it is an art that must be taught. For while it is an art, admitting of poetic weight, it is also an ordinary and rather prosaic craft that admits of ordinary discipline and ordinary prayer to shape it well. It takes both inspired discovery and careful plotting. And it is a craft that not only makes the one who practices it but also makes the church. Preaching can catch us up short well before we can take it in. So if the joined arts of composing sermons and listening to sermons *can't* be taught, how *must* they be taught?

About Other Books

There's a genre among books about preaching that roughly follows the old division between the theory of an art and the performing of an art. This genre of books lays out a few principles about what the interpretation and proclamation of biblical faith in the Christian sermon is meant to do. It then offers a few pointers toward how to do it. These are then followed by a number of sermons presented as examples embodying those principles and techniques. This is an approach that makes a certain sense. It holds on to a tension between study and experience. This tension goes back all the way to St. Augustine in the fourth century, and behind Augustine to the Roman schools of oratory led by Quintillian and the even earlier Greek theories of Aristotle. That tension can be found in the teaching of any art, not just the arts of preaching or other kinds of oratory. It is the tension between teachable rules meant to describe mastery and the knack or "practical wisdom" that cannot be taught like a list of rules. The knack can only be encouraged or teased out. The tried and true way of doing that is to create opportunities for active listening and experimentation. Teachers pray, cross their fingers, and depend on the innate ability of learners to apply to themselves what they hear. It places the teaching of an art smack between the hard-won achievement of reflection and the instinctive genius of a gift. And this goes for both creating art and receiving art, whether art is received by seeing or hearing.

That fourth-century North African divine Augustine was trained in the ancient art of persuasive speech called rhetoric. After his conversion, he committed himself to Christianizing that art for the sake of Christian preaching. The fourth "book," or chapter, of his *On Christian Doctrine* says it bluntly: as long as the spiritual maturity of the student of preaching is seriously attended to, the best way to learn is simply to listen to others preach with the skills of critical appreciation and self-application.[1] This means learning from what fails the church as well as from what serves it. And it means becoming not only a good hearer but a good reader too.

Now does this mean a teacher must work in the extremes, showing the "finest" examples of the craft and throwing in a few clunkers for fair warning? (This presumes, of course, that it is actually possible to decide which sermons are the finest or the worst.) Not necessarily. It is surely good to try on the robes of the occasional royalty of the art. There are preachers who seem crowned by the apparent effortlessness of their eloquence and the crowds that spontaneously gather in their hearing. And it is also chastening to encounter the best-laid plans gone awry in sermons that just don't deliver. Yet it may be as valuable to tend to more normally competent preachers too, and to develop a relationship with their preaching. By these I mean those preachers who rise from their congregations week by week to preach a word that slowly and carefully, over time, makes the church into a community in the face of the cross. These are the preachers who sermon by sermon preach a word that tends to Scripture as the source of life and opens hearts to the Holy Spirit. They make for more ordinary, and in so many ways more life-changing, hope in our churches.[2]

Another challenge working against simply transferring rules in the name of good preaching is the aspect of faithful speaking and hearing that extends through time. Preaching has more than a moment, you see. It has an arc that sometimes only reveals itself over the long haul. It is an arc hopefully bent toward life and goodwill, and it is colored by the many complications, challenges, joys, and discoveries of the very communities that house it. A prince or princess of the pulpit may be judged on the basis of one sermon, but a working pastor cannot. Judgment unfolds, week in and week out, in those cases. Novelty gives way to an eloquence that may be discovered only in the fruit it bears from season to season. So good listening is the counterpart to remembering the rules, and good listening includes variety as well as depth. It includes ongoing conversations with preachers one knows well, as well as going out of one's way to hear sermons from trustworthy strangers with foreign styles and surprising passions. The work of the student is in finding such voices and learning to pay attention, and that is not as simple as it sounds. The work of the teacher is to help.

About the Valuable Contingency of the Art

Consider that at the time of this writing there are 107 churches in the Chicago Presbytery of the Presbyterian Church (U.S.A.), which is but one regional body in but one of the group of old

Reformation denominations. Given the total membership of those churches and an assumption that roughly half of that total might be worshiping on any given Sunday, it is safe to say that somewhere between 17,000 and 20,000 Presbyterians are hearing sermons preached by 107 different preachers on any given Sunday in the Chicago area. Now by comparison, just down the road from one of those 107 churches is the quintessential example of what has come to be called a megachurch. This one independent congregation, called Willow Creek Community Church, in South Barrington, Illinois, lives in an odd and interesting relationship to churches like those 107. Were it Presbyterian, it alone would double the number of Presbyterians worshiping on any given Sunday in the Chicago area. Its lead pastor, Bill Hybels, is an effective preacher and a visionary in his own right. Whether one embraces or contests the value of his vision to Christ's church, or his theological correctness, one can still note the seriousness of purpose, discernible savvy, and sheer effectiveness of communication that has built that ministry.

My point in making the contrast between the 107 and the one is to note again that on any one of those given weekends there are roughly as many people worshiping in one church building in South Barrington listening to one sermon preached by one preacher as there are in 107 Presbyterian churches in 107 buildings listening, most likely, to 107 different preachers preach 107 different sermons. And each of those 108 sermons can as easily serve or fail the church as any other. There is no priviledged voice among them, except as measured by faithful rendering of the divine voice. Add to that the numbers of sermons preached on that same given Sunday in all of the other pulpits and congregations of all of the other denominational and nondenominational gatherings within shouting distance of those 108 churches, and you've got a lot of preaching going on. Now multiply to include the rest of the country and other parts of the globe: cathedral preaching, storefront evangelism, pastoral homilies, political gospels, exhortations for the mending of moral ways, outrageously extravagant claims, remarkably dry but surprisingly fruitful expositions of ancient texts, words of comfort, words of anger, expressions of joy, staid sermons and alive sermons, short ones and long, more in languages other than English than those in English, and preached to gatherings as small as ten to as large as ten thousand. Each sermon has a task to do and people to reach and a Scripture to serve and a hope to cling to. And each sermon has as much weight as the other, exemplary of the art or not. And each sermon plays with fire. Learning to preach, just as learning to hear preaching, begins in paying close, even very close attention to this diversity and to both the strange anomalies and wonderful discoveries this diversity displays.

I believe preaching remains the quintessential live, not recorded, rhetorical practice of our time, at least in those parts of the world still influenced by Christianity, Judaism, and Islam. And its sheer ubiquity and variety make it a practice quite difficult to define. So theoretical reflection on preaching, which teachers of preaching are wont to do, can rarely lead practice.

In the case of an art such as this, theory chases practice. It tries to grab the tail of the activity just long enough to decide if the activity is a tiger or a dinosaur. It then lets everyone know what it has decided, as if describing or defining practice is a way of controlling practice. The fact of it is that we can still only grab the tail. Or to shift the metaphor yet again, we encounter preaching a lot like the way one encounters the cross at St. Paul's Church. Preaching comes first. It insinuates its preemption into any attempt to theorize it. It's always already there, and that is the wonder of it.

This is why in this book I've reversed the usual priority of theory to practice. I've reversed the order so active listeners might read these chapters as they wish and take what reassurance, curiosity, or frustration from them that they will without feeling they're listening in on a classroom discussion. I've also reversed the order to make the point to those who attend to the art that thinking about preaching must begin in preaching itself. It therefore begins with hearers, a preacher being herself a hearer. Thus, thinking about preaching becomes thinking on the fly. It becomes a humble thinking, always deferring to others, allowing experiments, honoring the labor of working craftspeople, and respecting the otherness of the One to whom preaching is finally in service.

And so, a definition: *when enacted as a sermon, preaching is the liturgically situated, rhetorically disciplined, and passionately nonviolent witness to God's presence in Christ, God's love for the church and its people, and God's passion for all creation (persons, world, and cosmos alike) as these things are attested to in Scripture, interpreted by the Holy Spirit, and borne by the traditions of the faithful. In this, preaching is God's Word to a moment.*

Now, to break this definition apart.

A Sermon's Peculiar Task

Two practices of the early church warrant Christian preaching. One is the evangelistic speech of Peter, Paul, and the many early preachers who gave speeches in public settings telling the story of Jesus. They spoke to interpret the significance of Jesus in light of Hebrew Scripture, historical events, and the religious culture of the day.[3] This kind of preaching openly proclaimed the saving work of Christ in the world. It was usually coupled with a call to the hearers to affirm the truths proclaimed and to apply those truths to their lives, even to the point of mending their ways in light of these truths and joining with others who were doing the same. It was preaching to increase the church. Not primarily meant to interpret specific passages of Scripture or expound on emerging doctrines of the church, this kind of preaching brought the grab bag of the church's rhetorical resources (including Scripture) into a more general service. It was public oratory about Jesus adaptable to varied contexts and audiences. We can see it today in different forms of evangelistic preaching, the most active forms on television or radio.

The other practice is discovered in what we know of how the early church worshiped, adapting the synagogue form of public commentary on sacred texts to new purposes. This is what I call preaching in the form of a sermon. While less adaptable in some ways, the sermon actually carries a more complex function than more directed evangelistic speech. It is always part of a larger flow of worship that it both affects and is affected by. It is evangelistic, to be sure, at least when done well. It is also pedagogical in that it teaches those who have already made a commitment to the church about the Scripture and theology that has shaped the people of faith. It is also edifying, in that it is meant to deepen the faith of the gathered church. Yet it is also more.

Over time, the evangelical, pedagogical, and edification functions of the sermon came to be encompassed by the notion of exhortation, by which was meant the careful reminder to a people to acknowledge their common faith and align their lives according to what they already know.[4] They can know what they know either through the voice of their internal conscience or by repeating out loud what the church believes. "Remember your baptism, and be grateful" is a form of exhortation; so also is "Hear the Word of God." Such recollection is, at heart, what all preaching in the form of sermon is about.[5] This is why it is common, at least in a classically Reformed liturgy, for everyone to recite one of the historic creeds of the church (the Apostles' Creed, for example) either in preparation for hearing Scripture read and then preached on or shortly after the sermon has been preached. The congregation affirms that it is a community of common belief in the midst of diversity as a way of preparing to hear God's Word or as a way of confirming the Word it has heard interpreted.

A Sermon's Liturgical Situation

Liturgically situated in this way, the sermon is always both a response and a call. It is neither the first word of worship nor the final. The people gather in prayer and in praise of God, confess their sins to God and each other, accept words of forgiveness and encouragement, then hear a portion of Scripture read aloud, and sometimes affirm a creed. Then comes preaching, when enacted as a sermon.[6] To put it succinctly, a sermon is a rhetorical response to Scripture that has been prayed, sung, and read. It is imperfect by the imperfection of the person who offers it, but it is perfected by the actions and words to which it responds and which it prompts. It is offered as a gift by a person who has been called out of the pews to wrestle (with Scripture, the world, the Spirit, and so also the church) on behalf of those who are in the pews. That person is asked to come back from that wrestling to tell the tale. The preacher is in this sense commissioned to preserve the faith and complete the work of worship by doing something on behalf of others.

This is basically what the moment of preaching in the service is. It is the telling of tales of convergence where Scripture, the world, the Spirit, and so the church, meet. The sermon may be seven minutes or forty-seven minutes. It may be preached from a previously prepared manuscript or offered extemporaneously after much prayer and preparation of the preacher's spirit and mind. It may be offered by a preacher in vestments or merely holding a handkerchief to dry sweat from his brow. It may be intoned at volume or whispered as though a precious secret. No matter. It is still all this. And so it depends on a preacher as ready to hear as her congregation is ready to hear, and on a congregation as ready to respond as its preacher is ready to preach. It also depends on preachers and hearers trained well enough to know how to either minimize or forgive mistakes long enough to let insights be heard. And so it also depends, finally, on a movement in worship that clears space enough for a moment in which God's Spirit can lean in and down a bit, bringing these imperfect and sometimes all too human words closer to their truer, healing purpose. But more on this later.

A Sermon's Rhetorical Shaping

While I have insisted that preaching is liturgically situated, it is also rhetorically shaped. By this I mean that it is given form by human agency. While every preacher hopes, and some trust, that God will be at least a coparticipant in their preaching, every preacher—and most certainly every hearer—knows that a sermon is as much or more a human invention as it is a divine channeling. It is words discovered and made meaningful in delivery. It is designed with a persuasive purpose in mind and offered to a particular people in a particular place. And yet as much as it is certainly this, it is also something else. For given the wrestling I just described, sermons are more than simply one person trying to persuade a group of people about an idea he holds dear or an action she wants done. The persuasive intent of preaching is more complex because alongside practical ideas and specific actions a preacher may want a congregation to accept, the preacher is also inviting these hearers into a process of self-persuasion. In this self-persuasion, hearers either begin or continue their own conversations with the Spirit, the world, the Scripture, and the church. The preacher is a midwife to these conversations inside hearers and seeks to bring these conversations into responsive contact with the conversation going on inside of her as the preacher. She is inviting her congregation to overhear and join in.[7]

Sermons are given form to meet this purpose, and so must be open-ended enough, or loose enough, to both command attention and leave hearers turning not just toward the preacher but toward their own conscience, toward each other, and, most important, toward the Holy Spirit. The preacher preaches as the person he seeks to be before God, and preaches to his hearers imagining them to be the people they might best become before God. By doing this, preachers and congregations participate together in what God is doing in the world, particularly as they are taught what God is doing by the fourfold witness of Scripture, circumstance, the church through time, and the more mysterious inner witness of the Spirit. It is all a bit circular, but so it goes.

The Sermon's Wager on Nonviolence

All of this is the essence of the art. So it is here, in the way that the fourfold witness of Scripture, circumstance, church, and Spirit in the sermon comes together with that fourfold convergence of preacher, Scripture, world, and church that preaching makes a wager on nonviolence. For if I'm right in what I am saying about preaching, then there is something else about this worth thinking about: *the rhetorical form of preaching must express the character of the one whose voice a sermon means to make present.* It must begin to demonstrate in form and delivery a set of ideal expressions—of the preacher's character, the hearers' collective character, and the living character of Christ as known by the church. No easy task this. It is not as straightforward as coming up with a sermon statement and expanding it into an introduction, an argument, and a conclusion. And it is not as cut-and-paste as lifting one's arm a few degrees to the right whenever one says the word *Jesus* or following some other formula for getting the emotional response you want from your audience.

As to Christ's character, there are many ways to describe those aspects of his character a preacher might emulate, or hearers might seek. There is ample theological debate about the problem around. But to take my own license, I want to emphasize Christ's rejection of coercive violence. I believe this is important for preaching because preaching is so prone to manipulation and so easily a vehicle for rhetorical violence. By so implicating preaching in rhetorical violence I mean to describe something subtler than more obvious and all too prevalent forms of hateful speech. I mean to describe a manipulation that contradicts the gracious strength of Christ, even if it does so by accident. I mean to describe speaking that presumes too much and so takes away a hearer's freedom to respond. I mean speaking that steals a hearer's freedom of conscience and so steals the very space where the God of whom preaching preaches might speak in and to a hearer. Such preaching shouts God down, in the name of God, and so finally lies about God. Or, at best, it is left to be little more than gossip about God.

One example. For a short period after September 11, 2001, there was a great deal of American news-media attention given to preaching. Perhaps this was due in part to the notable increase in church attendance during the weeks after the al-Qaeda attacks. Perhaps media created part of the nation's thirst for an interpretive and comforting message and then insisted it was only reporting on it. We heard over and over again how unprecedented and earth-shattering those tragic events were, quite despite their sad familiarity to nations and peoples subjected too often to the many forms of terror that thrive in our world. In any case, there was a moment when much of the cultural anxiety that normally surrounds preaching seemed to melt.

I have nothing more than anecdotal evidence for this, but it is my strong impression that there was a confusing resonance to the pervasive use of "we" by preachers during those weeks. Any preacher's "we" was overladen with significance. Yet few preachers chose to define what they meant. The homiletic "we" seemed to slip without noticing among a "we" that refers to Christian people, a "we" that speaks of Americans, and another "we" that refers to a particular group of people gathered in a particular sanctuary. "We" were victims; "we" were crusaders, "we" were world-weighted burden-bearers. "We" were curious. "We" were angry—at Osama Bin Laden, at the American administration, at Saudis, at Palestinians, at God. To the extent that the "we" preached was not defined, I believe such preaching at such a time flirted with doing violence in the name of justice and healing. Given the task I assigned preaching just a moment ago, I believe the "we" of the preacher must be circumspect.

The "we" of the church includes its catholic expansiveness, drawing in all who worship throughout the world and throughout time. I cannot speak on behalf of the nation except as an aside. I can speak only on behalf of the church, and then with clarity regarding what I can and cannot say even about that. I believe the "we" of the church includes "I" and "you" into a radically different connection to others than the "we" most journalists were hoping the day's preachers would reassure. And yet this is part of the "we" that congregants brought into worship. It is not the preacher's task to ignore any "we" other than the "we" of the baptized. It is, rather, the preacher's task to bring the complex sets of identities we share with others into the consciousness of a congregation, and set that consciousness before the authority of the Scripture as it is carried by the "we" of the whole church. The preacher then lets that other authority judge, heal, and so free the identities brought in. This allows a new kind of "we" saying. Without this, we risk doing rhetorical violence even while trying so hard to avoid it.

Now a note of qualification to this is in order. When I mentioned to Timothy Hickey my suspicion that it is time to reaffirm the centrality of nonviolence in preaching, this pastor responsible for that leaning cross reminded me again that, while nonviolent in irrefutable ways, the cross does indeed intrude. He insisted that in the case of the sanctuary at St. Paul's Church, the only way to avoid the cross is to intentionally look away. So too in Christian preaching, he rightfully insisted. And the cross is a marker for a continuing and painful memory. There is a violence that attends a symbol such as the cross, for it is a symbol made from a tool of execution. Preaching rests on a continuum between an invitation given to the free and informed conscience of a hearer and an uncomfortable demand to wake up and hear. Healing sometimes takes some cutting. "If you've never heard a sermon that angers you, you've missed out on preaching," that one preacher said cryptically. The strength of restraint that allows a preacher to withhold certain enthusiasms in order to preserve a congregation's freedom to say no must be combined with a passion that communicates just as clearly that making no decision at all is no option. Nonviolence must not be confused with indifference.

The clue to the nonviolence I seek is in redirecting those dynamics of truth telling that in a violent world too often take on a violent aspect. This kind of truth telling makes absolute claims that, instead of breaking things down, breaks things open. It is a way of speaking that does not perpetuate a peace built on lies. It serves what is, finally, the only truly nonviolent act there is—divine, transforming love. This is love's truth. It can cut, but with an incision that bleeds not our blood but Christ's.

Nonviolent preaching still errs, for it never stops being as open to misstatement and misunderstanding as any human speech. Nevertheless, nonviolent preaching strives to *recognize* that it errs. It combines strong statement with the equally strong self-awareness that it is a broken vessel for an unbroken truth. It is on this that the integrity of the preacher hangs. Both the content and delivery of a sermon must show this.

Shifting Metaphors in the Pursuit of the Nonviolent Word

Imagine the sanctuary as a courtroom and the service of worship as a trial. It's easy to see a preacher as the advocate, or defense attorney, for what she sees to be the message she means to deliver. Seen this way, the sermon is a tactical move within God's strategy of defense. The preacher calls Scripture to the witness stand to testify on God's behalf and then cross-examines history and circumstance in the wake of Scripture's story. Preacher and congregation then see society as a prosecutor that has accused this gospel, and so the preacher launches his defense of this gospel through counteraccusation. If one follows this, then over against the church such preaching would place itself as a judge, ruling between what of the church sits on God's side of the courtroom and what of the church sits with the broken and aggressive world. In this view, hearers are, if anything, either members of the jury the preacher-attorney is addressing or the courtroom audience allowed to listen in on the transaction and occasionally being hushed to silence.[8]

I believe that while one can easily see the scene this way, preaching so imagined flirts with a kind of power that overwhelms the spiritual dimension of the preaching act. It presumes to see and know and say things it can't. This couldn't be farther from how the church has theologically affirmed the role of preaching through the ages. When positioned as if coming from sites of omniscience, strong homiletic statements become argumentative far too quickly and risk missing the fuller, continuous side of the truth they seek to serve. The strength of the sermon must first be found in the passionately nonviolent persistence I've just described, not in the force of a proposition or the histrionics of delivery. A preacher's propositions serve a different power than that sought by an accuser, defender, or judge. And a preacher's passion serves a different urgency than a drive to agreement through persuasive speech alone. Well-reasoned propositions and well-delivered convictions sooner appear as the products of a preacher having heard something she cannot but speak than they do the results of a preacher hell-bent on winning a case.

Holding on to the metaphor of the courtroom, despite its misuse, I want to imagine the pulpit less as an attorney's desk than as a witness stand. Surely the weakest of all places in the court, the witness stand is perhaps also the most pivotal. It is from the witness stand that the trial of truth can be made or broken. But the witness, of course, cannot control the outcome of the case, for the witness neither selects the questions and challenges nor makes final appeal to those who judge. The power of testimony rests on the integrity of character as revealed by the way in which a witness responds. It rests on her clarity, on the effect of her speech, on the wise hearing of jury and judge, and on the (liturgical) veracity of the courtroom. Witnesses speak of what they have struggled to see and recall and name, and they do so under another's examination and in a trial not their own. Again, others decide.

When offered as the testimony of a witness, the nonviolence of preaching need not be left in a sea of timidity. Preaching as nonviolent witness can speak with remarkable boldness without overwhelming the conscience and freedom of a faithful hearer. In both form and content, such preaching can help make a group of hearers into a community of faith responding to the trial of truth. It's a matter of speaking the sure knowledge of faith with assurance that it is not your accomplishment that makes it sure. And so you leave some work for hearers to do if they will, and you don't do harm to them if they won't. For they may yet. And it means remembering that the preacher is a hearer too.

Who then is the advocate in this trial of biblical and theological truth? At times perhaps the Holy Spirit. At other times perhaps the church's Scripture. At times perhaps history and circumstance. It surely depends, and these things cannot be so easily separated. So too with who might be positioned in the imagined world of the sermon as the judge. The judge metes out decisions, rewards, and punishments. The judge also works to keep the court fair, so others may judge justly. A preacher might want to take on that role, briefly, but he should always return to his position as witness and assure the court that he changes position only to serve the integrity of his testimony, not to presume the authority of another's place. Perhaps God is the judge, as God moves toward the sermon's hearers and calls them into a new world past the trial of truth.

Nonviolent Witness as Self-Application in Truth Telling

Consider two practices that make for the nonviolent witness I am seeking. The first practice is self-application, by which I mean two things—the learned ability to investigate one's life in the same way one investigates others' and the desire to apply to oneself and to the church the same measures one applies to the world. These being done, a preacher can begin to discern, and so describe, what difference Christ's story and Christ's presence might make. The second practice of nonviolent witness, then, is the cultivated art of telling the truth in love, which implies a rhetoric shaped by Christ's unwavering and involving compassion for the world.

In the echo of the example I just offered of preaching after September 11th, I believe that these practices call on us to rediscover both personal address in preaching and a new subjectivity. Here I return to that question of the homiletic "we." For I am advocating new ways of saying and hearing both "you" and "I." Indeed, many bluntly assume that personal address puts hearers off and sounds preachy, as if every "you" has a long, crooked finger pointing through it. Likewise, I hear many sermons studiously avoid the word "I" except in telling some story to illustrate a point. I take this to come from a reasonable desire not to appear self-conscious, self-righteous, or unsophisticated. And so sermons fall into the unclarified royal "we" I challenged earlier. This "we" is meant to communicate two things: first, that the preacher includes himself with the congregation and, second, that the individual hearers are, in fact, a community. But what if that "we" does the opposite and excludes more listeners than it includes by presuming others' experience before it ought? And what if a heartfelt "I believe" in preaching is basic to moving a preacher's speech from the implied attorney's desk to the implied witness stand? If this is so, then the preacher's courage in saying "I believe" might be vital to allowing the space for hearers to speak their own "I believe" in their own internal conversations—that is to say, as long as the preacher's "I believe" has behind it something like either the confession of the parent crying to Jesus on behalf of his demon-possessed child in Mark, "I believe, help my unbelief!" or the recognition of Paul when invited to defend his message before Agrippa. Paul testifies that his message is based not on knowledge but on a word to which he too is subject (Acts 26:22).

It should be stressed again that the "I believe" of the preacher is not simply the expression of an opinion. This subjectivity, like St. Paul's, retains the passion of having combined the achievement of reason with the receptivity of inspiration. It is the expression of a belief that is both constitutive of the preacher's very self and provisional before the greater wisdom of God. And it is the expression of a belief whose trustworthiness is earned through both the credibility of the preacher's life and the credibility of the divine life in Christ to which the preacher gives witness in believing. Similarly, might there not be a parallel use of "you" in preaching that frees others to hear a word that awakens their own subjectivity, replacing accusation with an invitation to conviction?

This is the subjectivity of Sir Thomas More in Robert Bolt's play *A Man for All Seasons*. There More stakes his defense of Catholic authority in the wake of Henry VIII's separation from Rome on making this kind of witness. When challenged by the

Duke of Norfolk over his assertion of the importance of apostolic succession to peaceful order in the church, he makes a statement that appears to make an argument about what *is* the case. He immediately repeats the statement, but through a simple shift in intonation he rephrases it as testimony rather than argument. When Norfolk retorts that Thomas is resting his view on merely a theory, More replies, "Why, it's a theory, yes; you can't see it; can't touch it; it's a theory. But what matters is not whether it's true or not but that I believe it to be true, or rather, not that I *believe* it, but that *I* believe it. . . . I trust I make myself obscure?"[9]

The distance between More and his friend widens as Thomas backs away from an instinct to insist that the verity of his belief is enough of an argument to warrant a claim on his friend's loyalty and insist on his friend's agreement: I believe it, so you should too. By positioning himself in relation to his actions in a way that implicates only himself, without implying privileged access to some universal knowledge, Thomas frees his interlocutor to remain in a responsive relationship even if his interlocutor disagrees. He thus invites his hearer to start a conversation in his own head about what he, his hearer, believes. Thomas thus invites his hearer to judge himself before the same court that he, Thomas, has placed himself. And Thomas does this without sacrificing his own freedom to make a strong claim, perhaps even a stronger claim than the one that rested solely on the logic of his belief. This is a "here I stand" lodged within the widening intrigues of faith.

Such a responsive subjectivity is not passive, because in order to avoid harming the other, it requires a listening sensibility on the part of a preacher that is rooted in the practice of self-application. My "I" must be open to other "I"s, and thus as open to being persuaded by just claims as it is passionate about claiming its own right to make just claims.

The irony here is that to common sense, More's second "I" speaks conviction in a way that may sound stronger and more domineering even though I am saying that it is in fact the most freeing of its hearer. I hinge my claim on its status as testimony, you see. For on the witness stand, one may be able to claim reason and make the strongest of assertions without doing harm both because one eschews control over the one to whom one is speaking and because one has made a prior public declaration of one's intention to avoid lying. But it should be noted again that what one eschews is control, not responsibility, obligation, or relation.[10]

This is not to suggest a complete preacherly moratorium on any "we" saying, for even the witness can speak on behalf of what she sees or knows of a collectivity. Consider this example: "We" the church have begun to see what the world has not yet seen. And "we" who are baptized are part of new reality, whether "you" and "I" fully grasp that reality or not. And so "you" may be challenged to decide to what "we" you should first give yourself—to a nation, a corporation, a class, a race, a gender, a sexual orientation, a family, or to Christ and the people claiming to be Christ's as they try to be church. Do we find our identity as a people, and do you find your identity as a person as part of the "we" of baptized people? Or do you find yourself, first, elsewhere? I believe Christ's Spirit would gently, but oh so firmly, place our baptism at the first.

This, I believe, is a "we" we can preach and a "you" you can hear. It is different, however, than a "we wonder where God is today." One "we" is the "we," and "you," and "I" of a multivoiced tradition, the other a "we" of a presumed unity. The distinction may appear obscure, but it presents itself with practice and makes all the difference in the world, I believe.

I believe myself commissioned to preach, and know others similarly commissioned to preach in a Spirit that transforms individuals and groups while never collapsing them one into the other. And it is this Spirit, so I believe I have heard, and so I trust, that is attested to in Scripture, interpreted by the same Spirit, and borne by the traditions of the faithful. The "I" that hearers hear and that preachers speak is not an "I" of retreat from scholarly precedent or ecclesial authority. Rather, it is an intentional positioning of oneself in relation to each of those things, and a bringing of that thicket of relations into an expectant relationship with the mysterious life of Christ's Spirit. It is the ground of hope against power and the gentle but insistent intrusion of a leaning cross that speaks without overwhelming and woos without the spell of charm or the harm of appeal to a presumably shared emotion.

About the Sermon as a Mending

So we come near to the end of my definition of preaching. To conclude this epilogue, I want to suggest another metaphor alongside witness by which one might consider the theological significance of preaching. It is healing, or mending, from the Hebrew word *tikkun*. Such mending has meanings beyond the repair of an individual body or a specific breach. It has lasting social, even cosmic, implications. It is the mending of the world.

German theologian Dietrich Bonhoeffer gave a series of lectures on preaching in the 1930s. He gave them in the small seminary dedicated to the training of pastors for that portion of the German church that refused the authority of the Nazi regime. Student notes from his lectures have been used to reconstruct his theology of preaching.[11] In those lectures, Pastor Bonhoeffer describes how the story of the original fall of humanity from its communion with God affects human speech. In our original brokenness, he says, we fall into the very brokenness we know in our daily speech, in which words and actions are too often severed.[12] We know the difference and the possibility of lying that comes with it. We are not who we say we are and cannot speak what we know most fully, and so we lose the very knowledge by which we might be what we are meant to be.

The separation lies at the very heart of how language means, for the word *tree* can evoke an image of a tree in the mind's eye only if the one who hears it or reads it knows that the word one hears or reads is not itself the tree it "speaks" of. In order to speak of the thing, the word cannot be the thing. And into that gap comes the potential for misstatement, misunderstanding, and confusion. And into this little break come the great fissures that tear us apart. For an imbalance of power enters this gap, so action invariably overpowers words. The quip "It's not what you say, it's what you do!" is a marker of our condition, according to Bonhoeffer. Pity poor words that fall prey to overpowering acts.

As strongly as an origin of our sin can be traced in the breach between word and action, the source of our hope as believing people is in the mending of that breach in Jesus Christ. For the church proclaims that in Jesus there was no such gap. With no separation between word and act in him, to participate in the Word of Christ is to participate in the mending of the world. And this preaching does. Preaching is as broken as all human speech, but like the ordinary bread and wine set apart by worship and sacramental language for an extraordinary purpose, so the sermon participates in the mending of all creation by testifying to the unity of word and act in Christ, as such unity is described in Scripture and effected in the world.

When the church calls Christ the Word of God it means to say that Christ is a word unlike any word we know. God in Christ is known to our intellect in the imperfect, broken way that any word "speaks" of that to which it is meant to refer. Yet Christ is God as the Word we seek, undivided. This Word is intimately, unequivocally, and eternally inseparable from that to which it refers. This Word is fully a part of what it speaks of and is, miraculously, still meaningful to us. Unrealizable in our world of broken speech, it is still the very hope by which we have confidence to speak at all. Therefore we speak, or better, we preach, in that hope. Such hope is itself the beginning of the more general mending that Bonhoeffer believes has both begun and will be completed one day in Christ. All worship testifies to the unity of words and actions in Christ, and the speaking and hearing of the preaching moment enacts it again. Hearers listen confident that every sermon is an echo, however faint, of Christ's healing Word.

This is a strong view of preaching, for it insists that preaching is not simply *about* God. It is, in its very act, a resonance *of* God. It restores the hope of healing, gives language to our long waiting for such healing, and strives to participate in the very mending it points to. This demonstrates why, from a strong theological point of view, preaching may never be separated from the transaction among preacher, church (universal and present), Scripture, and Holy Spirit that makes it. It is essentially dialogical. And here, again, is a description of how preaching is a dynamic, not passive, healing-while-revealing nonviolence. For it mends not by making a claim on its hearers for itself or for what it says, but it mends by making a claim on its hearers for the One to whom it gives witness. And it so serves by inspiring the imagination, transforming the will, and shaping the gathered community into a church engaging the world. It comes in the image of the very hope that heals the break and promises to give words to the great plenitude of creation that soothes the wounds that shatter.

The Speaking Spirit

When teaching a class in preaching, I once asked the dozen or so gathered to write on an index card an answer to a simple question: Why preach? More answers came back than were people in the class, for few could keep their responses to one reason. Many broke out along predictable lines. Methodists spoke of energizing hearts for service. Baptists spoke of persuading people to make decisions for Christ. Congregationalists spoke of their obligation to teach through the medium of the sermon and the importance of social transformation. Pentecostals spoke of inspiration and being a vehicle for the Holy Spirit filling the congregation. Some spoke of pastoral care. Two or three gave autobiographical answers, noting the occasions or words of advice from trusted others that had brought them to the edge of a preaching ministry. While we were listening to these and more responses, the parameters of a homegrown theology of preaching began to present themselves. That picture was presenting itself, at least, until we got to the final student in our circle. Kitty Liu turned her index card over and read aloud in a hesitating, almost embarrassed voice, "I preach because God is silent," she said. And everything turned. We spent the next several minutes and, truth be told, the rest of the semester working on the question she raised. I dare say each student, Kitty included, preached a bit differently because of the way Kitty's witness leaned into our discussion.[13]

Is God silent, after all? No. But is God silent in our day-to-day experience? Probably, at least in comparison with the noise of living. Then what does preaching do when it holds the paradox in its heart that God in Christ is the source of truth-telling, that God in Christ is plenitude and the very fullness of speech, that God in Christ is healing and true Word, and yet God in Christ is for most of us, most of the time, in a certain way silent? Our spiritual development may be more about learning to wait for God than counting up the times we feel God coming or hear God speaking. Our preaching, too, may become witness rather than argument to the extent that it knows it doesn't see all and know all. In other words, even as Christian preaching proclaims confidently that the violence of the cross is the liberation of all, it is Christian only to the extent that there is scored within that sure declaration a sense of yearning for the very God who dies on the cross to come again. We preach on Sunday, at the weekly feast of resurrection, but with the knowledge that empty Saturdays remain in our bones. Perhaps this is an answer to the reasonable challenge that a practice so generally flawed as real-life preaching couldn't possibly be the art of God's speaking. God speaks, even as God is also silent.[14]

How does preaching stand in the gap of this paradox, giving words to God's silence and so becoming God's Word without supplanting God or overthrowing human conscience? How to speak for God without speaking on God's behalf? How, simply, to speak in God's echo? However it is phrased, this is the question every preacher must ask as she or he begins to preach. And this may also be the very question that every hearer of good preaching must ask as well. For it is in the vigilant questioning that the answers begin to come.

The Holy Spirit gives words. As Paul of Tarsus once asked the church at Rome, "How then shall they call on him in whom they have not believed? And how shall they believe in him of whom they have not heard? And how shall they hear without a preacher?" (Rom. 10:14 KJV). They shall hear, as surely as the church calls women and men to preach and as surely as the cross keeps their preaching, and our hearing, Christian. And as surely as the historical violence of the cross meets us in preaching with a nonviolent but commanding witness to a healing Word.

So I believe.

Acknowledgments

As I noted in the epilogue, each of these chapters, except for the epilogue, began as a sermon. They now live in that odd space between sermons and essays. No sermon is a sermon if not delivered to a particular people in a particular place, but there's enough of a tradition in the church of lifting texts out of context and sharing them broadly to justify these approximations. As sermons, they were preached in some version or another in places as far afield as the First Presbyterian Church of Wilmette, Illinois, where I served as pastor in the late 1990s, Memorial Church at Harvard University, the Duke University Chapel, the Union church in Glencoe, Illinois, and Congregational churches in Woodbridge and Branford, Connecticut. Each of these congregations was gracious and patient. I must begin with thanks to them, particularly my hearers in Wilmette. They kindly survived my weekly preaching during the years I was their pastor. They gave me hope. It is, therefore, to the First Presbyterian Church of Wilmette and their new pastors that this book is dedicated.

I add thanks to my colleagues at Yale Divinity School for their challenge, support, and friendship, and for welcoming my teaching among them. I especially thank my senior preaching colleague, David Bartlett. I additionally thank folks at Brazos Press, particularly editorial director Rodney Clapp for his encouragement and wisdom and Rebecca Cooper for her editorial assistance. The press is a gift to the church, and so to the world. I thank the people whose stories I tell here, for their willingness and for their generosity. I thank my research assistants, Cathyann Plumer and John Thorpe. For reading early versions of various chapters, I thank Marthame and Elizabeth Sanders, Lillian Daniel, and David Wood. And for their gracious and wonderfully to the point editorial advice, I thank Mary Avram and Timothy Hickey. Strengths belong to all of these; mistakes belong to me. Finally, I thank my wife, Lynne, and my dear children, Andrew and Paul, for their love and faith.

An earlier version of chapter 5 appeared in the September-October 1999 issue of *Christian Ministry.* (Copyright 1999, Christian Century. Subscriptions: $49/yr. from P.O. Box 378, Mt. Morris, IL 61054. 1-800-208-4097.) It is reprinted by permission.

Notes

Introduction

1. Emmanuel Levinas, "The Trace of the Other," in *Deconstruction in Context: Literature and Philosophy*, ed. Mark C. Taylor (Chicago: University of Chicago Press, 1986), 354.

2. Evelyn Underhill, *The Way of the Spirit* (New York: Crossroad, 1990, repr.), 151.

The Heartbeat of Hope

1. Robert Inchausti, *The Ignorant Perfection of Ordinary People* (Albany, NY: SUNY Press, 1991), 74.

2. Christina Feldman and Jack Kornfield, *Stories of the Spirit, Stories of the Heart* (San Francisco: HarperSanFrancisco, 1991), 28–30. I'm grateful to Beldon Lane and Kristine Kerr for reference to this story.

God Then . . .

1. Denise Levertov, "Mass for the Day of St. Thomas Didymus," in *Candles in Babylon* (New York: New Directions, 1982). The poem is also anthologized in Susan A. Blain, ed., *Imaging the Word: An Arts and Lectionary Resource* (Cleveland: United Church Press, 1995), 2:121.

Jury Duty in the New Realm

1. C. S. Lewis, *The Great Divorce* (New York: Macmillan, 1945), 27–28.

9/12 Living in a 9/11 World

1. Hanna Rosin, "In Terror's Wake: 'God, You Around?'" *Washington Post*, September 27, 2001, A3.

No Wilder Peace

1. I share the story of Rabbi Jeremy Milgrom with permission.

2. Taken from an online letter, "The Listening Post," www.twelvedaystojeru salem.org/chacour/chacour.html. Text corrected for typographical errors.

3. I share this story with permission.

Blinded by the Light

1. C. Kirk Hadaway, "Denominational Defection: Recent Research on Religious Disaffiliation in America," in *The Mainstream Protestant "Decline": The Presbyterian Pattern*, eds. Milton J. Coalter, John M. Mulder, Louis B. Weeks, The Presbyterian Presence: The Twentieth-Century Experience (Louisville: John Knox, 1990), 102–21.

2. I share this story with permission.

3. To read more about the work of the Spirit in conviction-shaping experiences, see James E. Loder, *The Transforming Moment*, 2nd ed. (Colorado Springs: Helmers and Howard, 1989).

4. Morton T. Kelsey, *Prophetic Ministry: The Psychology and Spirituality of Pastoral Care* (New York: Crossroad, 1982), 70–71. Kelsey cites survey research done earlier by Andrew Greeley. While dated, common sense would suggest that the observation remains apt.

Against Heroes

1. Adapted from Søren Kierkegaard, *Attack Upon Christendom*, trans. Walter Lowrie (Boston: Beacon Press, 1956), 181.

On Martin Luther King Jr.: Self-Dispense or Self-Defense

1. Martin Luther King Jr., *Strength to Love*, 2nd ed. (Philadelphia: Fortress, 1981), 7.

2. Ibid., 151–52. For a stirring interpretation of this, see Inchausti's *Ignorant Perfection*, 77–94.

3. Stanley Hauerwas, *The Peaceable Kingdom* (Notre Dame, IN: University of Notre Dame Press, 1983).

4. Martin Luther King Jr., "Suffering and Faith," *Christian Century 77* (April 27, 1960): 510.

Gifts That Work

1. I share this story with permission.

Epilogue

1. Augustine, *Teaching Christianity (On Christian Doctrine)*, ed. John E. Rotelle, trans. Edmund Hill, in *The Works of Saint Augustine*, ed. John E. Rotelle, vol. 11, bk. 4, par. 2ff. (Hyde Park, NY: New City Press, 1990), 201ff.

2. If you are interested in this point, see Thomas G. Long, *The Witness of Preaching* (Louisville: Westminster/John Knox, 1989), 11–13.

3. For two of the earliest examples of Peter's preaching in Acts, one to a group of gathered believers and another to nonbelievers, see Acts 1:15–22 and Acts 2:14–36.

4. For a longer discussion of exhortation, see my article "Exhortation" in the *Encyclopedia of Rhetoric*, ed. Thomas O. Sloan (Oxford: Oxford University Press, 2001), 279–83.

5. See Ronald E. Osborn, *Folly of God: The Rise of Christian Preaching*, A History of Christian Preaching, vol. 1 (St. Louis: Chalice, 1999).

6. The order of worship described here is a classically Reformed one, in the Calvinist tradition that has influenced several Protestant traditions. It nevertheless carries over the Roman Catholic order of worship in large part, though one will find in some Anglican and Roman Catholic settings that the confession of sin, for example, comes after the Scripture has been interpreted in the sermon. In any of these cases, the sermon is still in response.

7. For a wonderful treatment of this, see Robin R. Meyers, *With Ears to Hear: Preaching as Self-Persuasion* (Cleveland: Pilgrim, 1993).

8. See Paul Ricoeur, "Hermeneutics of Testimony," in *Essays on Biblical Interpretation*, ed. with an introduction by Lewis S. Mudge (Philadelphia: Fortress, 1980), 119–20; John McClure, *Other-Wise Preaching: A Postmodern Ethic for Homiletics* (St. Louis: Chalice, 2001), esp. 97–132; Walter Brueggemann, *Cadences of Home: Preaching Among Exiles* (Louisville: Westminster/John Knox, 1997); Wes Avram, "Truth, Power, and Authority

in Rhetorical Theology," in *To Teach, to Delight, and to Move*, ed. David Cunningham, (Eugene, OR: Cascade Books, forthcoming).

9. Robert Bolt, *A Man for All Seasons: A Play in Two Acts* (New York: Random House, 1962), 91.

10. For another look at this, see my "Truth, Power, and Authority."

11. Dietrich Bonhoeffer, *Worldly Preaching: Lectures on Homiletics*, rev. ed., trans. Clyde E. Fant (New York: Crossroads, 1991); also see Frits DeLang, *Waiting for the Word: Dietrich Bonhoeffer on Speaking about God*, trans. Martin N. Walton (Grand Rapids: Eerdmans, 1993).

12. See Bonhoeffer, *Worldly Preaching*, esp. 102–4. Bonhoeffer elaborates on this in others of his writings. See, for example, *Christ the Center*, trans. Edwin H. Robertson (New York: Harper and Row, 1978), esp. 31.

13. I am grateful for permission to tell this story.

14. For a wonderful discussion of divine voice, see Stephen H. Webb, *The Divine Voice: Christian Proclamation and the Theology of Sound* (Grand Rapids: Brazos, 2004).